THE FORCE OF TRUTH

THE FORCE OF TRUTH

THOMAS SCOTT

THE BANNER OF TRUTH TRUST

THE BANNER OF TRUTH TRUST
3 Murrayfield Road, Edinburgh EH12 6EL
PO Box 621, Carlisle, Pennsylvania 17013, USA

*

First published 1779
First Banner of Truth edition 1984
ISBN 0 85151 425 1

*

Set in 10 on 11 ½ pt VIP Palatino
Typeset, printed and bound in Great Britain by
Hazell Watson & Viney Limited,
Member of the BPCC Group,
Aylesbury, Bucks

CONTENTS

PREFACE

TO THE SEVENTH EDITION*

ALMOST twenty years have now elapsed, since the ensuing Narrative was first published. During this time, the author has had abundant opportunities of examining, over and over again, the principles which he then intended to inculcate. If, therefore, he had, on further reflection, materially altered his sentiments, he should have thought himself bound, by the strongest obligations, to retract what he had erroneously advanced. But he is thankful that, on the contrary, he feels it incumbent on him to declare most solemnly, as in the presence of God, that everything which he has since experienced, observed, heard, and read, has concurred in establishing his most assured confidence, that the doctrines recommended in this publication are the grand and distinguishing peculiarities of genuine Christianity.

Very many verbal corrections, with a few retrenchments and additions, will be found in this edition. In improvements of this kind, the author has bestowed considerable pains: but he has been scrupulously, and almost superstitiously careful to admit no alteration which can in the least degree change the meaning of any passage.

He feels thankful, that the leading desire of his heart, in publishing a work which seems to relate almost exclusively to himself and his own little concerns, has not been wholly disappointed: but he would earnestly request the prayers of all who favour the doctrines he

* The first edition was dated Feb. 26, 1779, when the author was curate of Ravenstone and Weston Underwood, near Olney, Bucks.

inculcated, for a more abundant and extensive blessing on this, and all his other feeble endeavours to contend earnestly 'for the faith once delivered to the saints.'

Chapel-Street, Oct. 16, 1798.
Lothbury, London.

INTRODUCTION

In the past the author of these pages was principally known for his Commentary on the whole Bible, a work which involved him in massive labour and trouble and which in its day enjoyed an enormous circulation both in Great Britain and abroad. By the time of Scott's death copies to the value of £199,000 had been sold, £67,000 of English copies and £132,300 of American. These are of course enormous sums in equivalent modern currency. Unfortunately Thomas Scott's work, *The Force of Truth*, has fallen into obscurity in recent years. This is a great pity for it ranks among the best of short spiritual autobiographies.

The Force of Truth is valuable for three reasons. First of all, it is instructive. God says: 'I will bring the blind by a way that they knew not; I will lead them in paths that they have not known: I will make darkness light before them and crooked things straight. These things will I do unto them and not forsake them' (Isaiah 42:16). God's works in the lives of those he is determined to save are always instructive, and *The Force of Truth* is a particularly remarkable account of such a work. It is also interesting to note how slowly the work proceeded, with a gradual removal of erroneous principles and a slow emergence into the light of truth.

Secondly, the book has a warning for us. We are often prone to write people off as beyond hope of salvation. Saul of Tarsus before his conversion was held in the grip of false doctrine, a slave of sin and a vicious persecutor of God's people, yet God saved him. We profess that salvation is by grace, and so it is, but this means that the most depraved of sinners may be saved. Even professed ministers of the Gospel who have entered the ministry upon false grounds and hold to false teaching and are negligent of their duty may be saved by grace. The case of Thomas Scott supplies the reader with a warning not to limit the grace of God.

Thirdly, this account is immensely encouraging. There is force, there is power in the truth. The truth may be working in a man and yet we may know nothing about this. Certainly John Newton who was a great help to Scott recognised the power of the truth and was content to let Scott's spiritual development proceed unimpeded by human meddling.

It is difficult to believe that there is any evangelical minister or serious Christian who will fail to find benefit from this book, and who having read it, will not wish to return to it again and again. It supplies themes for meditation, feeds the soul, and will prove a real help in the communicating of truth to others.

*   *   *

Thomas Scott was born on 16th February, 1747. His place of birth was a small farmhouse at Braytoft in Lincolnshire; Braytoft is about six miles from the present town of Skegness. His father was a grazier (cattle farmer), and Scott was the tenth of thirteen children. At the age of ten he was sent to a boarding school at Scorton in Yorkshire where he remained for five years without returning home. Scott's eldest brother had been a surgeon's mate in the Royal Navy and would undoubtedly have become a surgeon had he not died of some disease at the age of twenty-four. His father wished Scott to follow in his brother's footsteps and thus in 1762 he was apprenticed to a surgeon and apothecary at Alford about eight miles from Braytoft. After two months, however, he was dismissed by his employer and due to a dispute over the payment of various fees, his employer refused to return his indentures. In consequence it became impossible for Scott to obtain employment with another surgeon and so his father's purposes were frustrated and the course of his own life was changed.

It is worth commenting at this juncture that Scott never lost his interest in medicine. When he became a curate in Buckinghamshire ten years later this interest manifested itself in a very practical way. 'About this time I began with great caution to administer medical assistance to a few of my poor neighbours and Mr (now Dr) Kerr of Northampton bestowed some pains in directing my proceedings, for he felt, as I have always done, that the poor in country villages are under great and pitiable disadvantages in this respect, which no humanity of their neighbours without medical skill, can prevent.' A few years later we learn of him labouring, at great risk to himself, to help those affected by smallpox and gaol fever in his parishes. We read: 'He had little confidence in the neighbouring apothecaries and none in the nurses . . . he called in Dr Kerr and "under him" he says "I was physician, apothecary, and almost nurse. I inoculated none, but some inoculated their neighbours, and I subsequently directed their proceedings." ' Dr Kerr was so impressed with Scott's medical talent that 'he frequently expressed a wish that he could change his profession; and would never himself give his directions to any other person when he was present.'

But we must return to Scott's earlier life. His dismissal by his employer necessarily meant that he had to work for his father as a grazier. In this situation he met with great hardship and incessant labour. Though he worked with immense diligence and considerable success he became increasingly embittered and thoroughly disgruntled with his lot. He began to study what books he had available and in April 1772 avowed his intention to his father of seeking ordination in the Church of England. It will be seen in the following pages that his motives for seeking entry into the ministry were of a most worldly kind. He tells us that the first of these was the desire for a less laborious way of getting his living than working upon a grazing farm. The next was the expectation that the clerical life would afford him more leisure for reading, which was the passion of his life. And lastly, he hoped that in due time he would distinguish himself as a literary man, as he felt within himself the capacity for success.

The spirit in which Scott entered upon the Christian ministry figures largely in the following pages but we must repeat here his memorable words on his ordination:

'As far as I understand such controversies, I was nearly a Socinian and Pelagian and wholly an Arminian: yet, to my shame be it spoken, I sought to obtain admission into the ministry, in a Church whose doctrines are diametrically opposed to all three ... While I was preparing for this solemn office, I lived as before in known sin, and in utter neglect of prayer ... Thus with a heart full of pride and wickedness, my life polluted with many unrepented, unforsaken sins; without one cry for mercy, one prayer for direction or assistance, or a blessing upon what I was about to do, after having concealed my real sentiments under the mask of general expressions, after having subscribed Articles directly contrary to what I believed, and after having blasphemously declared in the presence of God and of the congregation, in the most solemn manner, sealing it with the Lord's Supper, that I judged myself to be "inwardly moved by the Holy Ghost to take that office upon me" (not knowing or believing that there was a Holy Ghost), on 20th September, 1772, I was ordained a Deacon.'

In another place he writes of the same event:

'It suffices here to say, that, considered in all respects, I deliberately judge this whole transaction to have been the most atrocious wickedness of my life. But I did not, at that time, in any degree regard it in this light; nor did I, till long after, feel any remorse of conscience for my prevaricating, if not directly lying subscriptions and declarations, and all the evil of my motives and actions in the whole concern.'

In order to balance this comment we must add what he writes further:

'For ever blessed be the God of all long-suffering and mercy, who had patience with such a rebel and blasphemer, such an irreverent trifler with his majesty, and such a presumptuous intruder into his sacred ministry! I never think of this daring wickedness, without being filled with amazement that I am out of hell; without admiring that gracious God who permitted such an atrocious sinner to live, yea to serve him, and with acceptance, I trust, to call him Father, and as his minister to speak in his name.'

On his ordination Scott did not remain in Lincolnshire but became curate of two villages in Buckinghamshire, Stoke Goldington and Weston Underwood. It was whilst here that the great change recorded in *The Force of Truth* took place, and it was here that he first met John Newton, then minister in Olney. It was Newton's visit to two of Scott's dying parishioners which had a profound effect upon him. 'In January 1774 two of my parishioners, a man and his wife, lay at the point of death. I had heard of the circumstances, but according to my general custom, not being sent for, I took no notice of it; till one evening, the woman being now dead, and the man dying, I heard that my neighbour Mr Newton had been several times to visit them. Immediately my conscience reproached me with being shamefully negligent, in sitting at home within a few doors of dying persons, my general hearers, and never going to visit them . . . This reflection affected me so much, that without delay, and very earnestly, yea, with tears, I besought the Lord to forgive my past neglect.'

Scott had in fact already heard Newton preach and a remarkably disturbing experience it had proved to be. At the request of a friend he attended a Thursday evening meeting at Olney where Newton was the preacher. 'I sat fronting the pulpit and verily thought Mr Newton looked full on me when he came into the desk; and when he named his text, to my great astonishment it was this, "Then Saul (who also is called Paul) filled with the Holy Ghost, set his eyes on him, and said, O full of all subtlety and all mischief, thou child of the devil, thou enemy of all righteousness, wilt thou not cease to pervert the right ways of the Lord?" (Acts 13:9, 10). As I knew that he preached extempore, I took it for granted that he had chosen the text purposely on my account . . . I thought his doctrine abstruse, imaginative and irrational; and his manner uncouth; and the impression that, though Elymas was named, I was intended, abode with me for a long time: nor was it wholly effaced till I discovered some years afterwards that he was regularly expounding the Acts of the Apostles, and that this passage came in course that evening; and that, in fact, he neither saw nor thought of me.'

Another event of note during these years was his meeting with the lady who subsequently became his first wife. Scott relates that he first met with Mrs Jane Kell – obviously a widow – 'at a christening and won her money at cards.' It is recorded that the perfect composure and good temper with which she bore her loss was what deeply impressed Scott. Scott was blessed with an excellent wife and wrote to his sister of his wife that she 'seems to me to possess whatever can render woman amiable – beauty excepted: whom nature has blessed with a variety of her choicest gifts – sense, prudence, sensibility . . . who has many advantages of education, has read much, and is fit to appear with credit in any company, who has a heart fraught with most virtuous and generous sentiments . . . No woman in the world is better adapted for the management of a family.'

Scott was a man of great force of character, inflexible and of a somewhat fiery temper. His wife's good influence on him may be seen in two areas. 'She would say, "Only act according to the dictates of your conscience; we shall doubtless be provided for": yet, when she saw as she frequently did that my eager spirit and violent temper were hurrying me into wrong measures, she uniformly checked me, and though often not till after much opposition on my part, she always carried her point with me; to my unspeakable benefit. After I had written my sermons for the Sunday, I, for a long time, constantly read them to her before they were preached and, at her instance I altered many things, especially in exchanging words unintelligible to labourers and lace-makers, for simpler language.'

When John Newton left Olney for St Mary Woolnoth, London, in 1779, it was proposed that Scott should succeed him. This proposal excited violent opposition among the parishioners of Olney, which led to the proposal being dropped. But the curate chosen to replace

Newton turned out to be a veritable Tartar. Cowper says, 'He even quarrelled with his auctioneer in the midst of the sale of his goods and would not permit him to proceed, finishing that matter himself.' He is reported to have left his parishioners with the words, 'Now let us pray for your wicked vicar'. By that time those who had opposed Scott's coming to Olney had a change of heart and asked him to accept the now vacant situation. Scott in the end acceded to the request but his period at Olney was not to be a happy one. Writing about his situation at Olney in 1784 he says to a Scottish minister in the north of England:

'I am a moderate episcopalian and a paedobaptist; but I am entirely willing my brethren should be, some presbyterians, and some independents, and not extremely unwilling that some should be Baptists . . . There are above two thousand inhabitants in this town, almost all Calvinists, even the most debauched of them; the gospel having been preached among them for a number of years by a variety of preachers, statedly and occasionally, sound and unsound, in church and meeting. The inhabitants are become like David, wiser than their teachers; that is, they think themselves so, and in an awful manner have learned to abuse gospel notions to stupify their consciences, vindicate their sloth and wickedness, and shield off conviction.'

In 1785 Scott removed from Olney to London, to become chaplain to the Lock Hospital, or to give it its full title. 'The Lock Hospital for Persons Afflicted with the Venereal Disease'. His experiences at the Lock, his troubles and distresses, constitute a story in themselves. It is not possible to give a balanced view of his labours there in a short space. His labours among the inmates of the hospital, his preaching of Christ to them, and his attempts to help them to a better way of life through judicious practical measures, reveal Scott at his best. 'The reports drawn up by him, detailed many instances of those who were not only reclaimed and restored to society, but evidently converted to God by the means thus used; and who showed this by a long course of consistent conduct, terminating, in several cases, in a Christian and happy death.'

Scott's troubles originated with the aristocratic Board of Governors who controlled the Hospital and who were all divided by party spirit before Scott came. Also the aristocratic congregation, connected with the Hospital, did not take kindly to Scott's blunt preaching and close application of the truth. In their high views of divine sovereignty they were suspicious of exhortations to practical obedience.

We find him grappling with his difficulties as he lectured on Ephesians at his Wednesday night meetings: 'At first I was very well attended, my congregation generally consisting of more than three hundred persons. This continued while I was going through the more doctrinal part of the Epistle . . . When I arrived at the latter part of the fourth chapter, the alarm was spread, though I stamped every exhortation strongly with an evangelical seal. But at length, when I preached from the fifth chapter, on the words "See that ye walk circumspectly" etc, the charge was everywhere circulated that I had changed my principles and become an Arminian: and at once I irrecoverably lost much above half my audience.'

It must be remembered that Scott was an avowed Calvinist. He had become settled in his mind concerning the issues of the Arminian-Calvinist controversy years before. However the Governors of the Lock Hospital became very much troubled over Scott's emphasis on a Christian's *duties*, they being very zealous for what they

considered as 'Calvinism'. Scott preached a sermon on
Election and Perseverance in order to vindicate his
position. Furthermore at a large gathering of Governors
of the Lock, at which discussion was expected, he
proposed a question concerning the precise boundaries
between Calvinism and Arminianism. He writes of this
discussion: 'But in conference they added nothing unto
me: and, two dissenters excepted, no one offered anything sufficient to show that he understood the subject.
So that, when I concluded my own remarks, it was
allowed that I was more decidedly Calvinistic than the
rest of the company!' Some of the directors adopted an
authoritarian attitude in telling Scott what he ought to
preach, but he replied by saying, 'Gentlemen, you
possess authority sufficient to change me *for* another
preacher whenever you please but you have no power
to change me *into* another preacher'. He became very
discouraged and resolved to leave. But sharing this
determination with his wife he received the reply, 'Take
heed what you do; if you leave your station in this
spirit, you will perhaps soon be with Jonah in the
whale's belly'. As has already been noted, he seemed to
take much notice of what his wife said, and so he
retained his chaplaincy at the Lock Hospital.

Scott stayed at the Lock until 1801, undertaking many
and varied labours, including service as the first Secre-
tary of The Church Missionary Society. In September
1790 his wife died, which was the occasion of the
profoundest anguish to him. In 1791 he married again;
this marriage lasted for thirty years and 'was an
unspeakable blessing to him'.

We conclude this account of Scott's life in London
with a record of his Sunday labours, written by a
contemporary. 'At four o'clock in the morning of every
alternate Sunday, winter as well as summer, the watch-

man gave one heavy knock at the door and Mr Scott and an old maid servant arose – for he could not go out without his breakfast. He then set forth to meet a congregation at a Church in Lothbury, about three miles and a half off; I rather think the only church in London attended so early as six o'clock in the morning. I think he had from two to three hundred auditors, and administered the sacrament each time . . . From the City he returned home and about ten o'clock assembled his family to prayers: immediately after which he proceeded to the Chapel . . . His sermons were most ingeniously brought into an exact hour, just about the same time (as I have heard him say) being spent in composing them. I well remember accompanying him to the afternooon Church in Bread Street (nearly as far as Lothbury), after taking his dinner without sitting down . . . I have calculated that he could not go much less than fourteen miles in the day, frequently the whole of it on foot, besides the three services and at times a fourth sermon at Longacre Chapel, or elsewhere, on his way home in the evening; and then he concluded the whole with family prayer, and that not a very short one. Considering his bilious and asthmatic habit this was immense labour! And all this I knew him to do very soon after he had broken a rib by falling down the cabin stairs of a Margate packet; and it seemed to me as if he passed few weeks without taking an emetic! But his heart was in his work and I never saw a more devoted Christian.'

Here we must leave this outline of Scott's life. He left London shortly after the 19th Century opened and laboured at Aston Sandford in Buckinghamshire until his death in 1821. His first interests in the service of Christ remained with him till the last.

* * *

The Force of Truth by no means deals with the whole of Scott's Life. His Preface to the first edition was dated February 26, 1779, that is to say, shortly after his thirty-second birthday, while he was still curate at Ravenstone and Weston Underwood. Apart from the opening pages it covers only the first five years of his ministerial life. But these were the decisive years of his inner history for reasons which the author himself makes abundantly clear.

The year 1779, when this book first appeared, was also the year, it is interesting to note, when the youthful William Carey first met Scott. Years later in India Carey was to write of their friendship: 'If there be anything of the work of God in my soul, I owe much of it to his preaching, when I first set out in the ways of the Lord.'

This book is reprinted today with the prayer that it will encourage many others both to love the truth and to serve the Lord Jesus Christ.

John E Marshall
Hemel Hempstead, May 1984

FOR FURTHER READING

John Marshall, *Thomas Scott (1747–1821) and 'The Force of Truth'*, (Annual Lecture of the Evangelical Library, 1979).

John Scott, *The Life of Rev. Thomas Scott* (1822).

Thomas Scott, *Remarks on Bishop Tomline's Refutation of Calvinism* (1812).

PART ONE

An account of the state of the author's mind and conscience in the early part of his life, especially showing what his sentiments and conduct were, at the beginning of that change of which he proposes to give the history.

THOUGH I was not educated in what is commonly considered as ignorance of God and religion, yet, till the sixteenth year of my age, I do not remember that I ever was under any serious conviction of being a sinner, in danger of wrath, or in need of mercy; nor did I ever, during this part of my life, that I recollect, offer one hearty prayer to God in secret. Being alienated from God through the ignorance that was in me, I lived without him in the world, and as utterly neglected to pay him any voluntary service, as if I had been an atheist in principle.

But about my sixteenth year I began to see that I was a sinner. I was indeed a leper in every part, there being 'no health in me'; but out of many external indications of inward depravity, conscience discovered and reproached me with one especially; and I was, for the first time, disquieted with apprehensions of the wrath of an offended God. My attendance at the Lord's table was expected about the same time; and though I was very ignorant of the meaning and end of that sacred ordinance, yet this circumstance, uniting with the accusations of my conscience, brought an awe upon my spirits, and interrupted my before undisturbed course of sin.

Being, however, an utter stranger to the depravity and helplessness of fallen nature, I had no doubt that I could amend my life whenever I pleased. Previously therefore to communicating, I set about an unwilling reformation; and, procuring a form of prayer, I attempted to pay my secret addresses to the Majesty of heaven. Having in this manner silenced my conscience, I partook of the ordinance: I held my resolutions also, and continued my devotions, such as they were, for a short time: but they were a weariness and a task to me; and, temptations soon returning, I relapsed; so that my Prayer-book was thrown aside, and no more thought of, till my conscience was again alarmed by the next warning given for the celebration of the Lord's supper. Then the same ground was gone over again, and with the same issue. My goodness was like 'the morning-dew that passeth away'; and, loving sin and disrelishing religious duties as much as ever, I returned, as 'the sow that is washed, to her wallowing in the mire'.

With little variation, this was my course of life for nine years: but in that time I had such experience of my own weakness, and the superior force of temptation, that I secretly concluded reformation in my case to be impracticable. 'Can the Ethiopian change his skin, or the leopard his spots?' I was experimentally convinced that I was equally unable, with the feeble barrier of resolutions and endeavours, to stem the torrent of impetuous inclinations, when swelled by welcome, suitable, and powerful temptations; and being ignorant that God had reserved this to himself as his own work, and had engaged to do it for the poor sinner, who, feeling his own insufficiency, is heartily desirous to have it done by him, I stifled my convictions as well as I could, and put off my repentance to a more convenient season.

But, being of a reflecting turn, and much alone, my mind was almost constantly employed. Aware of the uncertainty of life, I was disquieted with continual apprehensions, that this more convenient season would never arrive; especially as, through an unconfirmed state of health, I had many warnings and near prospects of death and eternity. For a long time I entertained no doubt that impenitent sinners would be miserable for ever in hell: and at some seasons such amazing reflections upon this awful subject forced themselves into my mind, that I was overpowered by them, and my fears became intolerable. At such times my extemporary cries for mercy were so wrestling and persevering, that I was scarcely able to give over; though at others I lived without prayer of any sort. Yet, in my darkest hours, though my conscience was awakened to discover more and more sinfulness in my whole behaviour, there remained a hope that I should one day repent and turn unto God. If this hope was from myself, it was a horrid presumption; but the event makes me willing to acknowledge a persuasion that it was from the Lord: for had it not been for this hope, I would probably have given way to temptations, which frequently assaulted me, to put an end to my own life, in proud discontent with my lot in this world, and mad despair about another.

A hymn of Dr Watts (in his admirable little book for children), entitled 'The All-seeing God', at this time fell in my way: I was much affected with it, and, having committed it to memory, was frequently repeating it, and thus continually led to reflect on my guilt and danger. Parents may from this inconsiderable circumstance be reminded, that it is of great importance to store their children's memories with useful matter, instead of suffering them to be furnished with such corrupting trash as is commonly taught them. They know not what use God may make of these early rudiments of instruction in future life.

At this period, though I was the slave of sin, yet, my conscience not being pacified, and my principles not greatly corrupted, there seemed some hope concerning me; but at length Satan took a very effectual method of silencing my convictions, that I might sleep securely in my sins; and justly was I given over to a strong delusion to believe a lie, when I held the truth that I did know in unrighteousness. I met with a Socinian comment on the Scriptures, and greedily drank the poison, because it quieted my fears and flattered my abominable pride. The whole system coincided exactly with my inclinations and the state of my mind. In reading this exposition, sin seemed to lose its native ugliness, and to appear a very small and tolerable evil: man's imperfect obedience seemed to shine with an excellency almost divine; and God appeared so entirely and necessarily merciful, that he could not make any of his creatures miserable without contradicting his natural propensity.

These things influenced my mind so powerfully, that I was enabled to consider myself, notwithstanding a few little blemishes, as upon the whole a very worthy being. At the same time – the mysteries of the gospel being explained away, or brought down to the level of man's comprehension, by such proud and corrupt, though specious reasonings – by acceding to these sentiments, I was, in my own opinion, in point of understanding and discernment, exalted to a superiority above the generality of mankind; and I pleased myself in looking down with contempt upon such as were weak enough to believe the orthodox doctrines. Thus I generally soothed my conscience; and if at any time I was uneasy at the apprehension that I did not thoroughly deserve eternal happiness, and was not entirely fit for heaven, the same book afforded me a soft pillow on which to lull myself to sleep. It argued, and I then thought proved, that there were no eternal torments; and it insinuated that there were no torments except for notorious sinners, and that such as should just fall short of heaven would sink into their original nothing. With this welcome scheme I silenced all my fears, and told my accusing conscience that, if I fell short of heaven, I should be annihilated, and never be sensible of my loss.

By experience I am well acquainted with Satan's intention in employing so many of his servants to invent and propagate those pestilential errors, whether in speculation or practice, that have in all ages corrupted and enervated the pure and powerful doctrine of the gospel; for they lead to forgetfulness of God and security in sin, and are deadly poison to every soul that imbibes them, unless a miracle of grace prevent. Such, on the one hand, are all the superstitious doctrines of popery: purgatory, penances, absolutions, indulgences, merits of good works, and the acceptableness of will-worship and uncommanded observances; what are these but engines of the devil to keep men quiet in their sins? Man, resolved to follow the dictates of his depraved inclination, and not to bound his pursuits and enjoyments by the limits of God's holy law, catches at any thing to soften the horrible thought of eternal misery. This is the awakening reflection, God's sword in the conscience, which it is Satan's business, by all his diabolical artifices, to endeavour to sheath, blunt, or turn aside; knowing that while this alarming apprehension is present to the soul, he can never maintain possession of it in peace. By such inventions therefore as these, he takes care to furnish the sinner with that which he seeks, and to enable him to walk according to the course of this wicked world, and the desires of depraved nature, without being disturbed by such dreadful thoughts. The same, on the other hand, is the tendency of all those speculations of reasoning men, which set God's attributes at variance with one another; which represent the Supreme Governor as so weakly merciful, that he regards neither the demands of his justice, the glory of his holiness, the veracity of his Word, nor the peaceable order and subordination of the universe; which explain away all the mysteries of the gospel, and represent sin, that fruitful root of evil, that enemy of God, that favourite of Satan, as a very little thing, scarcely noticed by the Almighty, and which, contrary to the Scriptures and universal experience and observation, would persuade us that man is not a depraved creature.

To these latter sentiments I acceded, and maintained them as long as I could; and I did it, most assuredly, because they soothed my conscience, freed me from the intolerable fears of damnation, and enabled me to think favourably of myself. For these reasons alone, I loved and chose this ground: I fixed myself upon it, and there fortified myself by all the arguments and reasonings I could meet with. These things I wished to believe; and I had my wish; for at length I did most confidently believe them. Being taken captive in this snare of Satan, I should here have perished with a lie in my right hand, had not that Lord whom I dishonoured snatched me as a brand from the burning!

In this awful state of mind I attempted to obtain admission into holy orders! Wrapt up in the proud notion of the dignity of human nature, I had lost sight of the evil of sin, and thought little of my own sinfulness; I was filled with a self-important opinion of my own worth, and the depth of my understanding: and I had adopted a system of religion accommodated to that foolish pride, having almost wholly discarded mysteries from my creed, and regarding with sovereign contempt those who believed them. As far as I understood such controversies, I was nearly a Socinian and Pelagian, and wholly an Arminian:* yet, to my shame be it spoken, I sought to obtain admission into the ministry, in a church whose doctrines are diametrically opposed to all the three, without once concerning myself about those barriers which the wisdom of our forefathers has placed around her, purposely to prevent the intrusion of such dangerous heretics as I then was.

While I was preparing for this solemn office, I lived as before, in known sin, and in utter neglect of prayer: my whole preparation consisting of nothing else than an attention to those studies which were more immediately

* Possibly some readers may not fully understand the import of these terms: and for their benefit I would observe, that the Socinians consider Christ as a mere man, and his death merely as an example of patience, and a confirmation of his doctrine, and not as a real atonement satisfactory to Divine justice for man's sins. They deny the Deity and personality of the Holy Spirit, and do not admit that all Christians experience his renewing, sanctifying, and comforting influences; and they generally reject the doctrine of eternal punishments. The Pelagians deny original sin, and explain away the scriptural history of the fall of man. They do not allow the total depravity of human nature, but account for the wickedness of the world from bad examples, habits, and education. They suppose men to possess an ability, both natural and moral, of becoming pious and holy, without a new creation or regeneration of the heart by the Holy Spirit; and they contend for the freedom of the will, not only as constituting us voluntary agents, accountable for our conduct, but as it consists in exemption from the bondage of innate carnal propensities; so that man has in himself sufficient resources for his recovery to holiness by his own exertions. The Arminians deny the doctrines of gratuitous personal election to eternal life, and of the final perseverance of all true believers; and numbers of them hold the doctrine of justification by works, in part at least; and verge in some degree to the Pelagian system, in respect to the first moving cause in the conversion of sinners. (5th Ed.)

requisite for passing reputably through the previous examination.

Thus, with a heart full of pride and wickedness; my life polluted with many unrepented, unforsaken sins; without one cry for mercy, one prayer for direction or assistance, or a blessing upon what I was about to do; after having concealed my real sentiments under the mask of general expressions; after having subscribed Articles directly contrary to what I believed; and after having blasphemously declared, in the presence of God and of the congregation, in the most solemn manner, sealing it with the Lord's supper, that I judged myself to be 'inwardly moved by the Holy Ghost to take that office upon me'; (not knowing or believing that there was a Holy Ghost); on Sept. the 20th, 1772, I was ordained a Deacon.

For ever blessed be the God of all long-suffering and mercy, who had patience with such a rebel and blasphemer, such an irreverent trifler with his majesty, and such a presumptuous intruder into his sacred ministry! I never think of this daring wickedness without being filled with amazement that I am out of hell; without admiring that gracious God, who permitted such an atrocious sinner to live, yea, to serve him, and with acceptance, I trust, to call him Father, and as his minister to speak in his name. 'Bless the Lord, O my soul: and all that is within me, bless his holy name. Bless the Lord, O my soul, and forget not all his benefits: who forgiveth all thine iniquities; who healeth all thy diseases; who redeemeth thy life from destruction; who crowneth thee with loving-kindness and tender mercies.' May I love, and very humbly and devoutly serve that God, who has multiplied his mercies in abundantly pardoning my complicated provocations.

I had considerable difficulties to surmount in obtain-

ing admission into the ministry, arising from my peculiar circumstances; which likewise rendered my conduct
the more inexcusable: and my views, as far as I can
ascertain them, were these three: A desire of a less
laborious and more comfortable way of procuring a
livelihood, than otherwise I had the prospect of; the
expectation of more leisure to employ in reading, of
which I was inordinately fond; and a proud conceit of
my abilities, with a vainglorious imagination that I
should some time distinguish and advance myself in
the literary world. These were my ruling motives in
taking this bold step: motives as opposite to those which
should influence men to enter this sacred office, as pride
is opposite to humility, ambition to contentment in a
low estate, and a willingness to be the least of all and
the servant of all; as opposite as love of self, of the world,
of filthy lucre, and slothful ease, is to the love of God, of
souls, and of the laborious work of the ministry. To me
therefore be the shame of this heinous sin, and to God
be all the glory of overruling it for good, I trust, both to
unworthy me, and to his dear people, 'the church which
he hath purchased with his own blood'.

My subsequent conduct was suitable to these motives.
No sooner was I fixed in a curacy, than with close
application I sat down to the study of the learned
languages, and such other subjects as I considered most
needful, in order to lay the foundation of my future
advancement. And O that I were now as diligent in
serving God, as I was then in serving self and ambition!
I spared no pains, I shunned, as much as I well could, all
acquaintance and diversions, and retrenched from my
usual hours of sleep, that I might keep more closely to
this business. As a minister, I attended just enough to
the public duties of my station to support a decent
character, which I deemed subservient to my main

design; and, from the same principle, I aimed at the morality of my outward deportment, and affected seriousness in my conversation. As to the rest, I still lived in the practice of what I knew to be sinful, and in the entire neglect of all secret religion: if ever inclined to pray, conscious guilt stopped my mouth, and I seldom went further than 'God be merciful unto me!'

Perceiving, however, that my Socinian principles were very disreputable, and being conscious, from my own experience, that they were unfavourable to morality, I concealed them in a great measure, both for my credit's sake, and from a sort of desire I entertained (subservient to my main design), of successfully inculcating the practice of the moral duties upon those to whom I preached. My studies indeed lay very little in divinity; but this little all opposed that part of my scheme which respected the punishment of the wicked in the other world: and therefore (being now removed to a distance from those books whence I had imbibed my sentiments, and from the reasonings contained in them, by which I had learned to defend them), I began gradually to be shaken in my former confidence, and once more to be under some apprehension of eternal misery. Being also statedly employed, with the appearance of solemnity, in the public worship of God, whilst I neglected and provoked him in secret, my conscience clamorously reproached me with base hypocrisy: and I began to conclude that, if eternal torments were reserved for any sinners, I certainly should be one of the number. Thus I was again filled with anxious fears and terrifying alarms: especially as I was continually meditating upon what might be the awful consequence, should I be called hence by sudden death. Even my close application to study could not soothe my conscience nor quiet my fears; and, under the affected air of cheerfulness, I was truly miserable.

This was my state of mind when the change I am about to relate began to take place. How it commenced, in what manner and by what steps it proceeded, and how it was completed, will be the subject of the Second Part. I shall conclude this by observing that, though staggered in my favourite sentiment before mentioned, and though my views of the person of Christ were verging towards Arianism*; yet in my other opinions I was more confirmed than ever. What those opinions were, I have already briefly declared: and they will occur again, and be more fully explained, as I proceed to relate the manner in which I was constrained to renounce them, one after another, and to accede to those that were directly contrary to them. Let it suffice to say, that I was full of proud self-sufficiency, very positive, and very obstinate; and, being situated in the neighbourhood of those whom the world calls Methodists†, I joined in the prevailing sentiment; held them in sovereign contempt; spoke of them with derision; declaimed against them

* Arianism: the system of belief propagated by Arius (250–336 c.). He denied the Deity of Christ. The Athanasian Creed was drawn up to oppose his heresies.

† Methodist, as a stigma of reproach, was first applied to Mr Wesley, Mr Whitefield, and their followers; and to those who, professing an attachment to our established church, and disclaiming the name of dissenters, were not conformists in point of parochial order, but had separate seasons, places, and assemblies for worship. The term has since been extended by many to all persons, whether clergy or laity, who preach or profess the doctrines of the Reformation, as expressed in the Articles and liturgy of our church. For this fault they must all submit to bear the reproachful name, especially the ministers; nor will the most regular and peaceable compliance with the injunctions of the rubric exempt them from it, if they avow the authorized, but in a great measure exploded doctrines to which they have subscribed. My acquaintance hitherto has been solely with Methodists of the latter description, and I have them alone in view when I use the term.

from the pulpit, as persons full of bigotry, enthusiasm, and spiritual pride; laid heavy things to their charge; and endeavoured to prove the doctrines which I supposed them to hold (for I had never read their books) to be dishonourable to God and destructive to morality. And though in some companies I chose to conceal part of my sentiments, and in all affected to speak as a friend to universal toleration; yet, scarcely any person can be more proudly and violently prejudiced against both their persons and principles than I then was.

PART TWO

A history of the change which has taken place in the author's sentiments; with the manner in which, and the means by which, it was at length effected.

In January, 1774, two of my parishioners, a man and his wife, lay at the point of death. I had heard of the circumstance, but, according to my general custom, not being sent for, I took no notice of it; till one evening, the woman being now dead, and the man dying, I heard that my neighbour Mr Newton* had been several times to visit them. Immediately my conscience reproached me with being shamefully negligent, in sitting at home within a few doors of dying persons, my general hearers, and never going to visit them. Directly it occurred to me, that whatever contempt I might have for Mr Newton's doctrines, I must acknowledge his practice to be more consistent with the ministerial character than my own. He must have more zeal and love for souls than I had, or he would not have walked so far to visit, and supply my lack of care to those, who, as far as I was concerned, might have been left to perish in their sins.

This reflection affected me so much, that without delay, and very earnestly, yea, with tears, I besought the Lord to forgive my past neglect: and I resolved thenceforth to be more attentive to this duty; which resolution, though at first formed in ignorant dependence on my

* Mr Newton. John Newton, Curate of Olney (Bucks, 1764–80). Joint-author with William Cowper of the *Olney Hymns* (later became Rector of St Mary Woolnoth, London).

33

own strength, I have, by divine grace, been enabled hitherto to keep. I went immediately to visit the survivor; and the affecting sight of one person already dead, and another expiring, in the same chamber, served more deeply to impress my serious convictions: so that from that time I have constantly visited the sick of my parishes, as far as I have had opportunity; and have endeavoured, to the best of my knowledge, to perform that essential part of a parish minister's duty.

Some time after this, a friend recommended to my perusal the conclusion of Bishop Burnet's *History of his Own Time*, especially that part which respects the clergy. It had the intended effect: I was considerably instructed and impressed by it; I was convinced that my entrance into the ministry had been the result of very wrong motives, was preceded by a very unsuitable preparation, and accompanied with very improper conduct. Some uneasiness was also excited in my mind concerning my neglect of the important duties of that high calling: and, though I was enslaved by sin, and too much engaged in other studies, and in love with this present world, to relinquish my flattering pursuit of reputation and preferment, and change the course of my life, studies, and employments; yet, by intervals, I experienced desires and purposes, at some future period, of devoting myself wholly to the work of the ministry, in the manner to which he exhorts the clergy.

All these things increased the clamorous remonstrances of my conscience; and at this time I lived without any secret religion, because, without some reformation in my conduct, as a man and a minister, I did not dare to pray. My convictions would no longer be silenced or appeased, and they became so intolerably troublesome, that I resolved to make one more effort towards amendment. In good earnest, and not totally without seeking the assistance of the Lord by prayer, I now attempted to break the chains with which Satan had hitherto held my soul in bondage; and it pleased the Lord that I should obtain some considerable advantages. Part of my grosser defilements I was enabled to relinquish, and to enter upon a form of devotion. Formal enough indeed it was in some respects; for I neither knew that Mediator through whom, nor that Spirit by whom, prayers are offered with acceptance unto the Father: yet, though utterly in the dark as to the true and living way to the throne of grace, I am persuaded there were even then seasons when I was enabled to rise above a mere form, and to offer petitions so far spiritual, as to be accepted and answered.

I was now somewhat reformed in my outward conduct, but the 'renewing in the spirit of my mind', if begun, was scarcely discernible. As my life was externally less wicked and ungodly, my heart grew most proud; the idol self was the object of my adoration and obeisance; my worldly advancement was more eagerly sought than ever; some flattering prospects seemed to open, and I resolved to improve my advantages to the uttermost.

At the same time everything tended to increase my good opinion of myself; I was treated with kindness and friendship by persons, from whom I had no reason to expect it; my preaching was well received, my acquaintance seemed to be courted, and my foolish heart verily believed that all this and much more was due to my superior worth: while conscience, which, by its mortifying accusations, had been useful to preserve some sense of unworthiness in my mind, was now silenced, or seemed to authorize that pride which it had checked before. And having the disadvantage of conversing in general with persons who either favoured my sentiments, or who, from good manners, or because they saw it would be in vain, did not contradict me, I concluded that my scheme of doctrine was the exact standard of truth, and that by my superior abilities I was capable of confuting or convincing all who were otherwise minded. In this view of the matter, I felt an eager desire of entering into a religious controversy, especially with a Calvinist; for many resided in the neighbourhood, and I heard various reports concerning their tenets.

It was at this time that my correspondence with Mr Newton commenced. At a visitation, May, 1775, we exchanged a few words on a controverted subject, in the room among the clergy, which I believe drew many eyes upon us. At that time he prudently declined the discourse, but a day or two after he sent me a short note, with a little book for my perusal. This was the very thing I wanted: and I gladly embraced the opportunity which, according to my wishes, seemed now to offer; God knoweth, with no inconsiderable expectations that my arguments would prove irresistibly convincing, and that I should have the honour of rescuing a well-meaning person from his enthusiastical delusions.

I had indeed by this time conceived a very favourable opinion of him, and a sort of respect for him; being acquainted with the character he sustained even among some persons who expressed a disapprobation of his doctrines. They were forward to commend him as a benevolent, disinterested, inoffensive person, and a laborious minister. But, on the other hand, I looked upon his religious sentiments as rank fanaticism, and entertained a very contemptible opinion of his abilities, natural and acquired. Once I had had the curiosity to hear him preach; and, not understanding his sermon, I made a very great jest of it, where I could do it without giving offence. I had also read one of his publications;

but, for the same reason, I thought the greater part of it whimsical, paradoxical, and unintelligible.

Concealing, therefore, the true motives of my conduct under the offer of friendship, and a professed desire to know the truth (which, amidst all my self-sufficiency and prejudice, I trust the Lord had even then given me), with the greatest affectation of candour, and of a mind open to conviction, I wrote him a long letter; purposing to draw from him such an avowal and explanation of his sentiments, as might introduce a controversial discussion of our religious differences.

The event by no means answered my expectation. He returned a very friendly and long answer to my letter; in which he carefully avoided the mention of those doctrines which he knew would offend me. He declared that he believed me to be one who feared God, and was under the teaching of the Holy Spirit; that he gladly accepted my offer of friendship, and was no ways inclined to dictate to me; but that, leaving me to the guidance of the Lord, he would be glad, as occasion served, from time to time, to bear testimony to the truths of the gospel, and to communicate his sentiments to me on any subject, with all the confidence of friendship.

In this manner our correspondence began; and it was continued, in the interchange of nine or ten letters, till December the same year. Throughout I held my purpose, and he his. I made use of every endeavour to draw him into controversy, and filled my letters with definitions, inquiries, arguments, objections, and consequences, requiring explicit answers. He, on the other hand, shunned everything controversial as much as possible, and filled his letters with the most useful and least offensive instructions: except that now and then he dropped hints concerning the necessity, the true nature, and the efficacy of faith, and the manner in which it was to be sought and obtained; and concerning some other matters, suited, as he judged, to help me forward in my inquiry after truth. But they much offended my prejudices, afforded me matter of disputation, and at that time were of little use to me.

This, however, is certain, that through the whole of the correspondence, I disputed, with all the arguments I could devise, against almost everything which he advanced, and was very much nettled at many things that he asserted. I read a great part of his letters, and some books which he sent me, with much indifference and contempt. I construed his declining controversy into an acknowledgment of weakness, and triumphed in many companies as having confuted his arguments. And, finally, when I could not obtain my end, at my instance the correspondence was dropped.

His letters and my answers are now by me; and on a careful perusal of them, compared with all I can recollect concerning this matter, I give this as a faithful account of the correspondence. His letters will, I hope, shortly be made public, being such as promise greater advantage to others, than, through my proud, contentious spirit, I experienced from them. Mine deserve only to be forgotten, except as they are useful to me to remind me what I was, and to mortify my pride; as they illustrate my friend's patience and candour in so long bearing with my ignorance and arrogance; and notwithstanding my unteachable, quarrelsome temper, continuing his benevolent labours for my good; and especially as they remind me of the goodness of God, who, though he abominates and resists the proud, yet knows how to bring down the stout heart, not only by the iron rod of his wrath, but by the golden sceptre of his grace.

Thus our correspondence and acquaintance, for the present, were almost wholly broken off; for a long time we seldom met, and then only interchanged a few words on general topics of conversation. Yet he all along persevered in telling me, to my no small offence, that I should accede one day to his religious principles; that he had stood on my ground, and that I should stand on his: and he constantly informed his friends, that, though slowly, I was surely feeling my way to the knowledge of the truth. So clearly could he discern the dawnings of grace in my soul, amidst all the darkness of depraved nature, and my obstinate rebellion to the will of God!

This expectation was principally grounded on my conduct in the following circumstances: Immediately after the commencement of our correspondence, in May 1775, whilst my thoughts were much engrossed by some hopes of preferment; one Sunday, during the time of Divine service, when the psalm was named, I opened the Prayer-book to turn to it; but (accidentally shall I say, or providentially?) I opened upon the Articles of Religion; and the eighth, respecting the authority and warrant of the Athanasian Creed, immediately engaged my attention. My disbelief of the doctrine of a Trinity of co-equal persons in the unity of the Godhead, and my pretensions to candour, had both combined to excite my hatred to this Creed; for which reasons I had been accustomed to speak of it with contempt, and to neglect reading it officially. No sooner, therefore, did I read the words. 'That it was to be thoroughly received, and believed; for that it might be proved by most certain warrants of Holy Scripture,' than my mind was greatly impressed and affected. The matter of subscription immediately occurred to my thoughts; and from that moment I conceived such scruples about it, that, till my view of the whole system of gospel-doctrine was entirely changed, they remained insuperable.

It is wisely said by the son of Sirach, 'My son, if thou

come to serve the Lord, prepare thy soul for temptation.'* I had twice before subscribed these Articles, with
the same religious sentiments which I now entertained.
But conscience being asleep, and the service of the Lord
no part of my concern, I considered subscription as a
matter of course, a necessary form, and very little
troubled myself about it. But now, though I was greatly
influenced by pride, ambition, and the love of the world,
yet my heart was sincerely towards the Lord, and I
dared not to venture on a known sin, deliberately, for
the sake of temporal interest. Subscription to Articles
which I did not believe, paid as a price for church
preferment, I began to look upon as an impious lie, a
heinous guilt, that could never truly be repented of
without throwing back the wages of iniquity. The more
I pondered it, the more strenuously my conscience
protested against it. At length, after a violent conflict
between interest and conscience, I made known to my
patron my scruples, and my determination not to subscribe: thus my views of preferment were deliberately
given up, and with an increasing family I was left, as far
as mere human prudence could discern, with little other
prospect than that of poverty and distress. My objections
to the Articles were, as I now see, groundless: much self-
sufficiency, undue warmth of temper, and obstinacy,
were betrayed in the management of this affair, for
which I ought to be humbled; but my adherence to the
dictates of my conscience, and holding fast my integrity
in such trying circumstances, I never did, and I trust
never shall repent.

No sooner was my determination known, than I was
severely censured by many of my friends. They all, I am
sensible, did it from kindness, and they used arguments
of various kinds, none of which were suited to produce

* A quotation from the Apocrypha: Ecclesiasticus 2:1.

conviction. But, though I was confirmed in my resolution by the reasonings used to induce me to alter it, they at length were made instrumental in bringing me to this important determination: not so to believe what any man said, as to take it upon his authority; but to search the Word of God with this single intention, to discover whether the Articles of the Church of England in general, and this Creed in particular, were, or were not, agreeable to the Scriptures. I had studied them in some measure before, for the sake of becoming acquainted with the original languages, and in order thence to bring detached texts to support my own system; and I had a tolerable acquaintance with the historical and preceptive parts of them: but I had not searched this precious repository of divine knowledge, with the express design of discovering the truth in controverted matters of doctrine. I had very rarely been troubled with suspicions that I was or might be mistaken; and I now rather thought of becoming better qualified, upon scriptural grounds, to defend my determination, than of being led to any change of sentiments.

However, I set about the inquiry; and the first passage, as I remember, which made me suspect that I might be wrong, was James 1.5: 'If any of you lack wisdom, let him ask of God, that giveth to all men liberally, and upbraideth not; and it shall be given him.' On considering these words with some attention, I became conscious that, though I had thought myself wise, yet assuredly I had obtained none of my wisdom in this manner; for I had never offered one prayer to that effect during the whole course of my life. I also perceived that this text contained a suitable direction, and an encouraging promise, in my present inquiry; and from this time, in my poor manner, I began to ask God to give me this promised wisdom.

Shortly after, I meditated on, and preached from John 7.16, 17: 'My doctrine is not mine, but his that sent me. If any man will do his will, he shall know of the doctrine, whether it be of God, or whether I speak of myself.' I was surprised that I had not before attended to such remarkable words. I discovered that they contained a direction and a promise, calculated to serve as a clue in extricating the sincere inquirer after truth from that labyrinth of controversy in which, at his first setting out, he is likely to be bewildered. And though my mind was too much leavened with the pride of reasoning to reap that benefit from this precious text which it is capable of affording to the soul that is humbly willing to be taught of God, yet, being conscious that I was disposed to risk everything in doing what I thought his will, I was encouraged with the assurance, that if I were under a mistake, I should some time discover it.

I was further led to suspect that I might possibly be wrong, because I had not hitherto sought the truth in the proper manner, by attending to Proverbs 3.5, 6. 'Trust in the Lord with all thine heart; and lean not unto thine own understanding. In all thy ways acknowledge him, and he shall direct thy paths.' I could not but know that I had not hitherto trusted in the Lord with all my heart, nor acknowledged him in all my ways, nor depended on his directions in all my paths; but that, in my religious speculations, I had leaned wholly on my own understanding.

But though these and some other passages made for the present a great impression upon me, and influenced me to make it a part of my daily prayers, that I might be directed to a right understanding of the Word of God, yet my pride and addictedness to controversy had, as some desperate disease, infected my whole soul, and was not to be cured all at once. I was very far indeed from being a little child, sitting humbly and simply at the Lord's feet, to learn from him the very first rudiments of divine knowledge. I had yet no abiding suspicion, that all which I had heretofore accounted wisdom was foolishness, and must be unlearned and counted loss, before I could attain to the excellency of the true knowledge of Jesus Christ: for though I began to allow it probable that in some few matters I might have been in an error, yet I still was confident that in the main my scheme of doctrine was true.

Whenever I was too straitly pressed with objections and arguments against any of my sentiments, and when doubts began to arise in my mind, to put off the uneasiness occasioned by them, my constant practice was to recollect, as far as I could, all the reasonings and interpretations of Scripture on the other side of the question; and when this failed of affording satisfaction, I had recourse to controversial writings. This drew me aside from the pure Word of God, rendered me more remiss and formal in prayer, and furnished me with defensive armour against my convictions, with fuel for my passions, and food for my pride and self-sufficiency.

AUTHORS WHO INFLUENCED THOMAS SCOTT

At this time Locke's *Reasonableness of Christianity*, with his *Vindications* of it, became my favourite pieces of divinity. I studied this, and many other of Mr Locke's works, with great attention, and a sort of bigoted fondness; taking him almost implicitly for my master, adopting his conclusions, borrowing many of his arguments, and imbibing a dislike to such persons as would not agree with me in my partiality for him. This was of great disservice to me; as, instead of getting forward in my inquiry after truth, I thence collected more ingenious and specious arguments, with which to defend my mistakes.*

But one book which I read at this time, because mentioned with approbation by Mr Locke, was of singular use to me: this was Bishop Burnet's *Pastoral Care*. I found little in it that offended my prejudices, and many things which came home to my conscience respecting my ministerial obligations. I shall lay before the reader a few short extracts, which were most affecting to my own mind. Having mentioned the question proposed to those who are about to be ordained deacons, 'Do you trust that you are inwardly moved by the Holy Ghost to take upon you this office and ministry, to serve God for the promoting of his glory, and the edifying of his people?' he adds (page 111), 'Certainly the answer that is made to this ought to be well considered: for if any one says, "I trust so," that yet knows nothing of any such motion, and can give no account of it, he lies to the Holy Ghost, and makes his first approach to the altar with a lie in his mouth, and that not to men, but to God.' And again (page 112) 'Shall not he (God) reckon with those who dare to run without his mission, pretending that they trust they have it, when perhaps they understand not the importance of it; nay, and perhaps some laugh at it, as an enthusiastical question, who will yet go through with the office! They come to Christ for the loaves; they hope to live by the altar and

* After having spoken so freely of Mr Locke's divinity, which I once so highly esteemed, it seems but just to acknowledge the vast obligation which the whole religious world is under to that great man for his *Letters concerning Toleration* and his answers to those who wrote against them. The grounds of religious liberty, and the reason why everyone should be left to his own choice, to worship God according to his conscience, were, perhaps, never generally understood since the foundation of the world, till by these publications Mr Locke unanswerably made them manifest.

the gospel, how little soever they serve at the one, or preach the other; therefore they will say anything that is necessary for qualifying them to this, whether true or false.'

Again (page 122), having interwoven a great part of the excellent Office of the Ordination of Priests into his argument, concerning the importance and weight of the work of the ministry, he adds, 'Upon the whole matter, either this is all a piece of gross and impudent pageantry, dressed up in grave and lofty expressions, to strike upon the weaker part of mankind, and to furnish the rest with matter for their profane and impious scorn; or it must be confessed that priests come under the most formal and express engagements to constant and diligent labour, that can be possibly contrived or set forth in words.' He concludes this subject of the Ordination Offices, by exhorting all candidates for orders to read them frequently and attentively, during the time of their preparation; that they may be aware beforehand of the obligations they are about so solemnly to enter into, and to peruse them at least four times in a year, even after their ordination, to keep in their minds a continual remembrance of their important engagements.

How necessary this counsel is, every minister, or candidate for the ministry, must determine for himself; for my part, I had never once read through the Office when I was ordained, and was in great measure a stranger to the obligations I was about to enter into, till the very period; nor did I ever afterwards attend to it till this advice put me upon it. The shameful negligence and extreme absurdity of my conduct in this respect are too glaring not to be perceived with self-application by everyone who has been guilty of a similar omission. I would therefore only just mention, that hearty earnest prayer to God, for his guidance, help, and blessing, may

be suitably recommended, as a proper attendant on such
a perusal of our obligations.

Again, page 147, he thus speaks of a wicked clergyman: 'His whole life has been a course of hypocrisy in
the strictest sense of the word, which is the acting of a
part, and the counterfeiting another person. His sins
have in them all possible aggravations: they are against
knowledge, and against vows, and contrary to his
character: they carry in them a deliberate contempt of
all the truths and obligations of religion; and if he
perishes, he doth not perish alone, but carries a shoal
down with him, either of those who have perished in
ignorance through his neglect, or of those who have
been hardened in their sins through his ill example!'

Again (page 183), having copiously discoursed on the
studies befitting ministers, especially the study of the
Scriptures, he adds, 'But to give all these their full effect,
a priest that is much in his study ought to employ a
great part of his time in secret and fervent prayer for the
direction and blessing of God in his labours, for the
constant assistance of his Holy Spirit, and for a lively
sense of divine matters; that so he may feel the impressions of them grow deep and strong upon his thoughts;
this, and this only, will make him go on with his work
without wearying, and be always rejoicing in it.'

But the chief benefit which accrued to me from the
perusal was this: I was excited by it to an attentive
consideration of those passages of Scripture, that state
the obligations and duties of a minister, which hitherto
I had not observed, or to which I had very loosely
attended. In particular (it is yet fresh in my memory), I
was greatly affected with considering the charge of
precious souls committed to me, and the awful account
one day to be rendered of them, in meditating on Ezekiel
33.7–9: 'So thou, O son of man, I have set thee a

watchman unto the house of Israel; therefore thou shalt hear the word at my mouth, and warn them from me. When I say unto the wicked, O wicked man, thou shalt surely die; if thou dost not speak to warn the wicked from his way, that wicked man shall die in his iniquity; but his blood will I require at thine hand. Nevertheless, if thou warn the wicked of his way to turn from it; if he do not turn from his way, he shall die in his iniquity; but thou hast delivered thy soul.' For I was fully convinced with Bishop Burnet, that every minister is as much concerned in this solemn warning as the prophet himself.

Acts 20.17–35, was another portion of Scripture, which, by means of this book, was brought home to my conscience; especially verses 26–28, which serve as an illustration of the preceding Scripture. 'Wherefore I take you to record this day, that I am pure from the blood of all men. For I have not shunned to declare unto you all the counsel of God. Take heed therefore unto yourselves, and to all the flock, over the which the Holy Ghost hath made you overseers, to feed the church of God, which he hath purchased with his own blood.'

In short, I was put upon the attentive and repeated perusal of the Epistles to Timothy and Titus, as containing the sum of a minister's duty in all ages. I searched out, and carefully considered, every text I could find in the whole Scripture, which referred to this argument. I was greatly impressed by 1 Corinthians 9.16: 'For necessity is laid upon me; yea, woe is unto me, if I preach not the gospel!' Nor was I less struck with Colossians 4.17: 'Say to Archippus, Take heed to the ministry which thou hast received in the Lord, that thou fulfil it.' This was brought to my conscience with power, as if the apostle had in person spoken the words to me. But especially I was both instructed and encouraged by meditating upon I Peter 5.2–4: 'Feed the flock of God which is among you, taking the oversight thereof, not by constraint, but willingly; not for filthy lucre, but of a ready mind; neither as being lords over God's heritage, but being ensamples to the flock. And when the chief Shepherd shall appear, ye shall receive a crown of glory that fadeth not away.'

I hope the reader will excuse my prolixity in speaking on this subject, because in itself it is very important. And though I obtained no new views of gospel truth from Burnet's *Pastoral Care*, yet I received such a deep conviction of the difficulty and importance of that work in which I had thoughtlessly engaged, and of the imminent danger to which my soul would be exposed, should I neglect to devote myself wholly to it, as laid the foundation of all my subsequent conduct and change of sentiments. I was, indeed, guilty of very criminal procrastination, after I had been thus convinced; and, being engaged more than I ought in other matters, I for some time postponed and neglected complying with the dictates of my conscience. But I never lost sight of the instruction I had received, nor ever enjoyed any comfortable reflection, till, having broken off all other engagements, I had given myself up to those studies and duties which pertain to the work of the ministry. And I have cause to bless God that this book ever came in my way.

Still, however, my self-confidence was very little abated, and I had made no progress in acquiring the knowledge of the truth. I next read Tillotson's *Sermons* and Jortin's *Works*; and, my time being otherwise engaged, I for a while gave in to the indolent custom of transcribing their discourses with some alterations, to preach to my people. This precluded free meditation on the Word of God, and led me to take up my opinions on trust. My preaching was in general that smooth, palatable mixture of law and gospel, which corrupts both by representing the gospel as a mitigated law, and as accepting sincere instead of perfect obedience. This system, by flattering pride and prejudice, and soothing the conscience, pleases the careless sinner and self-righteous formalist, but does real good to none; and is in fact a specious and unsuspected kind of antinomianism.*

About this time I foolishly engaged in a course of diversion and visiting, more than I had done since my ordination. This unfitted me for secret prayer and close meditation, and rendered the Scriptures and other religious studies insipid and irksome to me, a never-failing consequence of every vain compliance with the world. For a season, therefore, my ardour was damped, my anxiety banished, and my inquiries retarded. I was not, however, permitted entirely to drop my religious pursuits: generally I made it a rule to read something in the Scriptures every day, and to perform a task of daily devotion; but in both I was very formal and lifeless.

Yet, not long after, I was engaged in earnest meditation on our Lord's discourse with Nicodemus (John's Gospel, chapter 3). I felt an anxious desire to understand this interesting portion of Scripture; especially to know what it was to be 'born again,' or 'born of the Spirit,' which in five verses our Saviour has three times declared absolutely necessary to salvation. I was convinced it was absurd to suppose that such strong expressions implied no more than baptism with water. Tillotson's controversial sermons on this subject afforded me no satisfaction. Some great and total change I supposed to be intended, not only in the behaviour, but also in the heart. But not

* 'Against law': a general name for the belief that Christians are by grace delivered from the obligation to observe any moral law.

having clearly experienced that change, I could not understand in what it consisted. However, having offered some poor prayers for divine teaching, I undertook to preach upon it; but I talked very darkly, employed a considerable part of my time in declaiming against visionaries and enthusiasts, and reaped very little benefit from it. Yet I was so well satisfied with my performance, that, in the course of my correspondence with Mr Newton, I sent him these sermons for his perusal; and he, in return, sent me some of his own upon the same subject. But, though sincerely desirous to understand our Lord's meaning in this important point, I was too proud to be taught by him: I cast my eye therefore carelessly over some of them, and returned the manuscript, without closely attending to anything contained in it.

Nothing material occurred after this, till the next spring, 1776; when I was induced, by what I had learned from Bishop Burnet, to establish a lecture once a week in one of my parishes for expounding the Scriptures. This brought many passages, which I had not before observed, under attentive consideration; and afforded my reflecting mind abundance of employment, in attempting to reconcile them with one another, and with my scheme of doctrine.

Little progress however had been made, when, in May, 1777, I heard a dignified clergyman, in a visitation sermon, recommend Mr Soame Jenyns' *View of the Internal Evidence of the Christian Religion*. In consequence of this recommendation, I perused it, and not without profit. The truth and importance of the gospel revelation appeared with convincing evidence to my understanding, and came with efficacy to my heart by reading this book. I received from it more distinct, heart-affecting views of the design of God in this revelation of himself, than I had before; and I was put upon much serious reflection and earnest prayer to be led to, or established in the truth, concerning the nature and reality of the atonement by the death of Christ: for hitherto I had been, in this respect, a Socinian, or very little better.

But to counterbalance this advantage, Dr Clarke's *Scriptural Doctrine of the Trinity*, and the controversy which ensued upon its publication, became a favourite part of my study. The Arian scheme is so inconsistent with reason, that when reflecting men, in order to avoid those mysterious, and, as they imagine, unreasonable conclusions, which, according to the true meaning of words, the Scriptures contain, have become Arians, it is wonderful they do not, for the same cause, embrace the Socinian system. This is the natural progress of unhumbled reason; from Arianism to Socinianism; from Socinianism to Deism; and thence to Atheism. Many and awful have been the examples of reasoning and learned men, who, under the name of philosophers, arrogating to themselves the prerogative of superior discernment, have manifested the propriety with which they claimed this pre-eminence, by treading this down-hill road, almost, if not quite, to the very bottom.

But when a man has fallen so low as Socinianism, not merely for want of information, or by blindly and implicitly adopting the sentiments of other men, but by leaning to his own understanding, and preferring the conclusions of his own reason to the infallible dictates of the Holy Ghost, it is not common for him to return gradually, by the retrograde path, first to Arianism, and then to the received doctrine of the Trinity. Yet this was my case. Dr Clarke appeared to me so undeniably to establish his argument by express scriptural evidences, and so plausibly to defend his system on both sides, and to back his cause with so many seeming authorities, that I found myself unable any longer to maintain my Socinian principles, and was constrained to relinquish them as untenable: at the same time I was not aware of the flaw in his reasoning, and the unavoidable conse-quence of his middle doctrine; namely, 'that the Son and Holy Spirit, however exalted or dignified with names and titles, must either be mere creatures, or that otherwise there must be three Gods'. Not perceiving this, and my newly-acquired reverence for Scripture, and my old self-confidence and fondness for reasoning being, by this conciliating scheme, both humoured, I cordially acceded to his sentiments, and for a long time could not endure any other doctrine.

Nothing further of any consequence occurred till about December 1776, when carelessly taking up Mr Law's *Serious Call*, a book I had hitherto treated with contempt, I had no sooner opened it, than I was struck with the originality of the work, and the spirit and force of argument with which it is written. I mean merely as to his management of the subjects he treats of: for there are many things in it that I am very far from approving; and it certainly contains as little gospel as any religious work I am acquainted with. But though a very uncomfortable book to a person who is brought under a serious concern for his soul, and deep convictions of sin, it is very useful to prepare the way, to show the need we have of a Saviour, and to enforce the practice of that holy diligence in the use of means which the important interests of eternity reasonably demand. This was its use to me. By the perusal of it, I was convinced that I was guilty of great remissness and negligence; that the duties of secret devotion called for far more of my time and attention than had been hitherto allotted to them; and that, if I hoped to save my own soul, and the souls of those that heard me, I must in this respect greatly alter my conduct, and increase my diligence in seeking and serving the Lord. From that time I began to study in what manner my devotions might be rendered more fervent and pertinent; I transcribed, and committed to memory, scriptural petitions; I employed some time in reading manuals of devotion; made attempts to compose prayers myself, and became more frequent and earnest, and, I trust, more spiritual, than heretofore, in my secret addresses to the Majesty of heaven.

About this time, after many delays, I complied with the admonitions of my conscience, and disengaged myself from all other employments, with a solemn resolution to leave my temporal concerns in the hands of the Lord, and entirely to devote myself to the work of the ministry. Being thus become master of all my time, I dropped every other study, and turned the whole current of my reflections and inquiries into another channel; and for several years I scarcely opened a book which treated of anything besides religion.

The first step I took after this disengagement was to keep common-place books; one I had for noting down remarkable passages out of other authors; and another for collecting into one view every text I could meet with in Scripture respecting the most important and controverted doctrines of the gospel. Though I held this but a short time (for when my engagements multiplied I dropped it), yet I found it very useful in bringing me acquainted with many passages of the Word of God, to which I had not hitherto much attended; and it prepared the way for writing my sermons on doctrinal subjects, with the scriptural testimonies concerning the point in hand, in one view before me.

In January 1777, I met with a very high commendation of Mr Hooker's writings, in which the honourable appellation of Judicious was bestowed upon him. This excited my curiosity to read his works, which accordingly I did with great profit. In his *Discourse on Justification*, (edit. 1682, p. 469), I met with the following remarkable passage, which as well for its excellency as for the effect it had upon my religious views, I shall, though rather long, transcribe.

'If our hands did never offer violence to our brethren, a bloody thought doth prove us murderers before him [God]. If we had never opened our mouth to utter any scandalous, offensive, or hurtful word, the cry of our secret cogitations is heard in the ears of God. If we did not commit the sins which, daily and hourly, in deed, word, or thought, we do commit, yet, in the good things which we do, how many defects are there intermingled! God, in that which is done, respecteth the mind and intention of the doer. Cut off then all those things wherein we have regarded our own glory; those things which men do to please men, and to satisfy our own liking; those things which we do by any respect, not sincerely and purely for the love of God; and a small score will serve for the number of our righteous deeds. Let the holiest and best thing we do be now considered: we are never better affected unto God than when we pray; yet when we pray, how are our affections many times distracted! how little reverence do we show unto the grand Majesty of God unto whom we speak! how little remorse of our own miseries! how little taste of the sweet influence of his tender mercies do we feel! Are we not as unwilling many times to begin, and as glad to make an end, as if, in saying, "Call upon me," he had set us a very burdensome task?

'It may seem somewhat extreme which I will speak; therefore let everyone judge of it, even as his own heart shall tell him, and no otherwise. I will but only make a demand: if God should yield unto us, not, as unto

Abraham, if fifty, thirty, twenty, yea, or if ten good persons could be found in a city, for their sakes the city should not be destroyed; but and if he should make us an offer thus large: Search all the generations of men, since the fall of our father Adam; find one man that hath done one action, which hath passed from him pure, without any stain or blemish at all; and for that one only man's action, neither men nor angels shall feel the torments which are prepared for both: do you think that this ransom to deliver men and angels could be found to be among the sons of men? The best things which we do have somewhat in them to be pardoned; how then can we do anything meritorious or worthy to be rewarded? Indeed, God doth liberally promise whatso-ever appertaineth to a blessed life, to as many as sincerely keep his law, though they be not exactly able to keep it. Wherefore we acknowledge a dutiful necessity of doing well, but the meritorious dignity of doing well we utterly renounce. We see how far we are from the perfect righteousness of the law; the little fruit which we have in holiness, it is, God knoweth, corrupt and unsound; we put no confidence at all in it; we challenge nothing in the world for it; we dare not call God to reckoning, as if we had him in our debt-books. Our continual suit to him is, and must be, to bear with our infirmities, and pardon our offences.'

I had no sooner read this passage, than I acquired such an insight into the strictness and spirituality of the divine law, and the perfection which a just and holy God, according to that law, cannot but require in all the services of his reasonable creatures, that I clearly per-ceived my very best duties, on which my main depend-ence had hitherto been placed, to be merely specious sins, and my whole life appeared to be one continued series of transgression. I now understood the apostle's meaning, when he affirms, that 'By the works of the law can no flesh be justified before God.' All my difficulties in this matter vanished; all my distinctions and reasonings about the meaning of the words 'law' and 'justification', with all my borrowed criticisms upon them, failed me at once. I could no longer be thus amused; for I was convinced, beyond the possibility of a doubt, that all men were so notoriously transgressors of every law of God, that no man could possibly be justified in his sight by his obedience to any of the divine commandments. I was sensible that if God should call me into judgment before him, according to the strictness of his perfect law, for the best duty I ever performed, and for nothing else, I must be condemned as a transgressor; for when weighed in these exact balances, it would be found wanting.

Thus I was effectually convinced, that if ever I were saved, it must be in some way of unmerited mercy and grace, though I did not clearly understand in what way till long after. Immediately, therefore, I took for my next text, Galatians 3.22. 'But the scripture hath concluded all under sin, that the promise by faith of Jesus Christ might be given to them that believe.' And I preached from it according to Hooker's doctrine; expressing, as strongly as I could, the defilements of our best actions, and our need of mercy in everything we do, in order the more evidently to show that 'salvation is of grace, through faith; not of works, lest any man should boast'.

I had not, however, as yet attained to a knowledge of the fulness of that fountain, whence all these polluted streams flow forth so plentifully into our lives and conversation. Neither was I then able to receive the following nervous passage concerning justification, (Hooker, page 495): 'The righteousness wherein we must be found, if we will be justified, is not our own;

therefore we cannot be justified by any inherent quality. Christ hath merited righteousness for as many as are found in him. In him God findeth us, if we be faithful; for by faith we are incorporated into Christ. Then, although in ourselves we be altogether sinful and unrighteous, yet even the man which is impious in himself, full of iniquity, full of sin; him, being found in Christ through faith, and having his sin remitted through repentance, him God beholdeth with a gracious eye; putteth away his sin by not imputing it; taketh quite away the punishment due thereunto by pardoning it; and accepteth him in Jesus Christ as perfectly righteous as if he had fulfilled all that was commanded in the law. Shall I say, more perfectly righteous than if himself had fulfilled the whole law? I must take heed what I say; but the apostle saith, 'God made Him to be sin for us, who knew no sin, that we might be made the righteousness of God in him.' Such we are in the sight of God the Father, as the very Son of God himself. Let it be counted folly, or frenzy, or fury, whatsoever, it is our comfort, and our wisdom; we care for no knowledge in the world but this, that man hath sinned, and God hath suffered; that God hath made himself the Son of man, and that men are made the righteousness of God.'

Equally determinate and expressive are these words, (page 500): 'As for such as hold, with the Church of Rome, that we cannot be saved by Christ alone without works, they do, not only by a circle of consequences, but directly, deny the foundation of faith; they hold it not, no, not so much as by a thread.' If the judicious Hooker's judgment may in this important concern be depended upon (and I suppose it will not easily be proved erroneous), I fear the foundation of faith is held by only a small part of that church which has honoured her champion with this distinction.

In pages 508 and 509, he thus defends his doctrine against the objections of the papists (for at that time none but the papists openly objected to it): 'It is a childish cavil wherewith, in the matter of justification, our adversaries do so greatly please themselves, exclaiming, that we tread all Christian virtues under our feet, and require nothing of Christians but faith; because we teach that faith alone justifieth. Whereas, by this speech, we never meant to exclude either hope or charity from being always joined as inseparable mates with faith in the man that is justified; or works from being added, as necessary duties, required at the hands of every justified man: but to show that faith is the only hand which putteth on Christ unto justification; and Christ the only garment, which being so put on, covereth the shame of our defiled natures, hideth the imperfections of our works, preserveth us blameless in the sight of God; before whom, otherwise, the weakness of our faith were cause sufficient to make us culpable; yea, to shut us out from the kingdom of heaven, where nothing that is not absolute can enter.'

Had I at this time met with such passages in the writings of the dissenters, or in any of those modern publications which, under the brand of Methodistical, are condemned without reading, or perused with invincible prejudice, I should not have thought them worth regard, but should have rejected them as wild enthusiasm. But I knew that Hooker was deemed perfectly orthodox, and a standard writer, by the prelates of the church in his own days. I learned from his dispute with Mr Travers, that he was put upon his defence, for making concessions in this matter to the Church of Rome, which the zealous Protestants did not think warrantable; and that he was judged by the more rigid too lax in his doctrine, by none too rigid. I had never heard it insinuated that he was tinctured with enthusiasm; and the solidity of his judgment, and the acuteness of this reasoning faculties, need no voucher to the attentive reader. His opinion, therefore, carried great weight with it, made me suspect the truth of my former sentiments, and put me upon serious inquiries and deep meditation on this subject, accompanied with earnest prayers for the teaching and direction of the Lord on this important point. The result was, that after many objections and doubts, and much examination of the Word of God, in a few months I began to accede to Mr Hooker's sentiments. And at the present, my opinion, in this respect, as far as I know, coincides with these passages of this eminent author and is supported and vindicated by the same arguments. He, therefore, who would prove our doctrine of justification by faith alone to be an error, will do well to answer in the first place these quotations from Mr Hooker.

Indeed, as far as I can understand him, there is scarcely any doctrine which, with no inconsiderable offence, I now preach, that is not as evidently contained in his writings as in my sermons. Witness particularly his *Sermon of the Certainty and Perpetuity of Faith in the Elect*, in which the doctrine of the final perseverance of true believers, is expressly taught and scripturally maintained: and he closes it with this noble triumph of full assurance, as resulting from that comfortable doctrine in the hearts of confirmed and experienced Christians: 'I know in whom I have believed; I am not ignorant whose precious blood has been shed for me; I have a Shepherd full of kindness, full of care, and full of power: unto him I commit myself. His own finger hath engraven this sentence on the tables of my heart: "Satan hath desired to winnow thee as wheat, but I have prayed that thy faith fail not." Therefore, the assurance of my hope

I will labour to keep as a jewel unto the end, and by labour, through the gracious mediation of his prayer, I shall keep it.' (Page 532). With such words in my mouth, and such assurance in my heart, I wish to live, and hope to die.

The insertion of these quotations from this old author will, I hope, need no apology. Many have not his works, and these extracts are worthy of their perusal; others, from these specimens, may be prevailed with to read what perhaps hath hitherto been an unnoticed book in their studies. Especially I recommend to those who admire him as the champion of external order and discipline of the church, and who willingly allow him the honour of being distinguished by the epithet Judicious, that they would attentively read, and impartially consider his doctrine. This would put an effectual stop to those declamations that, either ignorantly or maliciously, are made against the very doctrines as novel inventions, which have just now been explained and defended in Mr Hooker's own words. For my part, though I acknowledge that he advances many things I should be unwilling to subscribe, yet, I heartily bless God that at this time I read him, the first material alteration that took place in my views of the gospel being in consequence of it.

One more quotation I shall make, and so take my leave of him. Addressing himself (in his second *Sermon on part of St Jude's Epistle*) to the pastors who are appointed to feed the chosen in Israel, he says (page 552), 'If there be any feeling of Christ, any drop of heavenly dew, or any spark of God's good Spirit within you, stir it up; be careful to build and edify, first yourselves, and then your flocks in this most holy faith. I say, first yourselves; for he who will set the hearts of other men on fire with the love of Christ, must himself

burn with love. It is want of faith in ourselves, my
brethren, which makes us retchless (careless) in building
others. We forsake the Lord's inheritance, and feed it
not. What is the reason of this? Our own desires are
settled where they should not be. We ourselves are like
those women who have a longing to eat coals, and lime,
and filth: we are fed, some with honour, some with ease,
some with wealth: the gospel waxeth loathsome and
unpleasant in our taste: how should we then have a care
to feed others with that which we cannot fancy ourselves? If faith wax cold and slender in the heart of the
prophet, it will soon perish from the ears of the people.'

It is not needful to add any reflections upon this
homely, searching passage; everyone will readily make
them for himself: we are however reminded of Sol-
omon's words, 'There is no new thing under the sun. Is
there any thing whereof it may be said, See, this is new?
It hath been already of old time, which was before us'
(Eccl. 1.9, 10). 'That which hath been is now; and that
which is to be hath already been' (Eccl. 3.15).

To my shame be it spoken, though I had twice
subscribed the Articles, which allow the Book of Homilies to be sound and wholesome doctrine, I had never
yet seen them and understood not what that doctrine
was. But being at length engaged in a serious inquiry
after truth, and Hooker's Works having given me a more
favourable opinion of these old authors, I was inclined
to examine them, and I read part of the book with some
degree of attention. And though many things seemed
hard sayings that I could not receive; yet others were
made very useful to me, especially concerning justification. In short, I perceived that the very doctrine, which
I had hitherto despised as Methodistical, was indisput-
ably the standard doctrine of the Established Church,
when the homilies were composed; and consequently

that it is so still; for they have lost none of their authority (however fallen into disrepute) with those who sub- scribe the Thirty-nine Articles. This weakened my prejudice, though it did not prove the doctrine true.

A CHANGE IN SCOTT'S PREACHING AND ITS EFFECTS

About this time a new and unexpected effect was produced by my preaching. I had hitherto been satisfied to see people regularly frequent the church, listen attentively to what was discoursed, and lead moral, decent lives. The way in which I had been led was so smooth, and the progress I had made so gradual; I had lately experienced so little distressing concern for my own soul, and had so little acquaintance with persons conversant in these matters; that while I declared the strictness, spirituality, and sanction of the law of God in an alarming manner, it never occurred to me that my hearers might not proceed in the same easy, gradual way. But I had scarcely begun this new method of preaching, when application was made to me by persons in great distress about their souls; for, their consciences being awakened to a sense of their lost condition by nature and practice, they were anxious in inquiring what they must do to be saved. I knew not well what to say to them, my views being greatly clouded, and my sentiments concerning justification very much per- plexed: but, being willing to give them the best counsel I could, I exhorted them in a general way to believe in the Lord Jesus Christ; though I was incapable of instruct- ing them either concerning the true nature of faith, or in what manner they were to seek it. However, I better understood my own meaning, when I advised them to the study of the Scriptures, accompanied with prayer to God to be enabled rightly to understand them, and when

I inculcated amendment of life. In this manner the Lord slowly brought them forward: and though, for want of a better instructor, they were a considerable time before they arrived at establishment in the faith; yet some of them, having their minds less leavened with prejudice and the pride of reasoning, were more apt scholars in the school of Christ than I was, and got the start of me in the knowledge both of doctrine and duty; and in their turns became, without intending it, in some respects monitors to me, and I derived important advantage from them.

The singular circumstance, of being an instrument in bringing others earnestly and successfully to inquire after salvation, while I so little understood the true gospel of Jesus Christ, very much increased my perplexity. I became doubly earnest to know the truth, lest I should mislead those who confided their precious souls to me as their spiritual instructor. This added to my diligence in reading and meditating on the Word of God; and made me more fervent in prayer to be guided to the knowledge of the truth. And under every difficulty, I constantly had recourse unto the Lord, to preserve me from ignorance and error, and to enable me to distinguish between the doctrines of his Word and the inventions and traditions of men.

About this time I established a weekly lecture for expounding the Scriptures in my other parish, by which I obtained further acquaintance with the various parts of the Word of God. It was my general practice, in penning these lectures, to search out all the texts referred to in the margin of the Bible, with such as I could recollect upon the subject and to make use of them in comparing one with another. This method enabled me to store my memory with the language of Scripture; and made way for a greater exactness in discussing doctrinal subjects than I had hitherto been acquainted with.

In the course of the winter, 1777, I was engaged in deep meditation upon Luke 11.9–13, concerning the Holy Spirit being given in answer to prayer. And at length, having made a collection of all the scriptures I could meet with, which related to that important doctrine, diligently comparing them together, and meditating upon them, and earnestly beseeching the Lord to fulfil the promise to my soul, I wrote two sermons upon the subject: one from Luke 11.13, 'If ye then, being evil, know how to give good gifts unto your children: how much more shall your heavenly Father give the Holy Spirit to them that ask him?' The other from James 1.16, 17: 'Do not err, my beloved brethren. Every good gift and every perfect gift is from above, and cometh down from the Father of lights.' By this, my views of a Christian's privileges and duties in this respect, were much enlarged, and my requests were made known unto the Lord in a more full, exact, and believing manner, than before. Though I still remained very ignorant in many important matters respecting the person, offices, and work of the Holy Spirit, yet I had discovered more of what was promised concerning him, and therefore knew better what to ask.

My obligations to Bishop Beveridge must here be acknowledged. When I first began to peruse his sermons, I conceived a mean opinion of him; and it was some time before I could prevail with myself to examine any further into his writings: but being now more advanced in my inquiry after truth, those singularities which at first offended me became tolerable, and I began to relish the simplicity, spirituality, love of Christ, and affection for souls, which eminently shine forth in many parts of his works. Indeed, I received considerable instruction from him; but especially his sermon on the real satisfaction made by the death of Christ for the sins of believers was the blessed means of clearing up my views and confirming my faith, respecting that fundamental doctrine of Christianity. On Good Friday, 1777, I preached a sermon upon that subject, from Isaiah 53.6: 'All we like sheep have gone astray; we have turned every one to his own way; and the Lord hath laid [hath caused to meet] on him the iniquities of us all.' I endeavoured to prove (what has ever since been the sole foundation of all my hopes), that Christ indeed bore the sins of all who should ever truly believe, in all their guilt, condemnation, and deserved punishment, in his own body on the tree. I explicitly avowed my belief, that Christ, as our Surety and Bondsman, stood in our lawplace, to answer all our obligations, and to satisfy divine justice and the demands of the law for our offences: and I publicly renounced, as erroneous and grievous perversions of Scripture, all my former explanations and interpretations of these subjects.

This was the first doctrine in which I was clearly and fully brought to acknowledge the truth; though I had, with no little earnestness, for two years been inquiring about it – to so astonishing a degree was my blinded understanding filled with prejudice against the doctrines of the Word of God! Hitherto they had been foolishness to me; but now, under the divine teaching, I began, though very dimly, to discern the wisdom of God in them.

I say dimly; for I was still under many and great mistakes, and very ignorant in many important points. I knew sin to be the transgression of the divine law; but I did not perceive its odious deformity, as deliberate rebellion against God's sovereign authority, and an express contradiction to his holy nature; as charging

God foolishly, with the want of either wisdom or goodness, in laying such restraints upon the inclinations of his creatures; and as tending to overturn all subordination in the universe, and to introduce anarchy, confusion, and misery into the whole creation. I had discovered that my best actions were defiled; but I understood not that this was the effect of a depraved nature and a polluted heart. The doctrine of original sin, as the fruitful root of these multiplied evils, was as yet no part of my creed. Inconsistently, I was an Arian, or a Clarkist, in my sentiments concerning the person of Christ and the divinity of the Holy Ghost. Some faint conception I had formed of the sanctifying work of the Holy Spirit in the soul. The beginnings of it I little understood: and I continued to entertain an implacable enmity to the doctrine of election, and the truths more intimately connected with it. But my faith was now fixed upon a crucified Saviour (though I dishonoured his person, and denied his Deity), and I had a sincere desire of being devoted to the Lord. He therefore in mercy accepted his own work in my heart, and pardoned all that was mine; and at length extricated me from that labyrinth of perplexities and inconsistences in which I was entangled.

About this time, in the course of my lectures, our Lord's discourse with Nicodemus came again under my consideration. Notwithstanding much meditation and many prayers, I could not satisfy my mind about it. I was convinced some internal change must be implied in the expressions 'born again', and 'born of the Spirit'; and, according to what I had experienced, I endeavoured to explain it; but I was still very confused in my views of that important subject, and had many doubts whether I were right or wrong in what I advanced.

Hitherto, excepting Leland's *Deists and their Writings*, I

had not read any book written by a dissenter, with the least degree of candour and attention; but at this crisis I met with the first volume of Dr Evans' sermons entitled *The Christian Temper*. I was induced to read it by the recommendation of a friend; but (such was my proud foolish heart!) I opened it with great prejudice, because I understood that the author was a dissenter. However, this book came with a blessing: for by perusing it, I at length perceived that fallen man, both body and soul, is indeed carnal and sold under sin; that by nature, in every man living, the reasonable and immortal part is destitute of spirituality, immersed in matter, and, by a dishonourable and miserable prostitution, given up 'to make provision for the flesh, to fulfil the lust thereof'; and, that man must be renewed in the spirit of his mind, new created unto good works, born of the Spirit of God, made partaker of a new and divine nature, before he can possibly be made meet for, or admitted into the kingdom of God. In a very little time all my difficulties about this matter vanished, and the truth became so exceedingly plain and evident, that, until I had made the experiment, I could scarcely be persuaded, but that every person who heard it rightly explained must assent to it. This doctrine I have ever since invariably preached, with good effect, I trust, in opening the eyes of sinners, and turning them 'from darkness to light, and from the power of Satan unto God' (Acts 26.18).

When I had made this little progress in seeking the truth, my acquaintance with Mr Newton was resumed. From the conclusion of our correspondence in December 1775, till April 1777, it had been almost wholly dropped. To speak plainly, I did not care for his company; I did not mean to make any use of him as an instructor; and I was unwilling the world should think us in any way connected. But under discouraging circumstances, I had

occasion to call upon him; and his discourse so com-
forted and edified me, that my heart, being by his means
relieved from its burden, became susceptible of affection
for him. From that time I was inwardly pleased to have
him for my friend, though not, as now, rejoiced to call
him so. I had, however, even at that time, no thoughts
of learning doctrinal truth from him, and was ashamed
to be detected in his company; but I sometimes stole
away to spend an hour with him. About the same
period, I once heard him preach; but still it was foolishness to me, his sermon being principally upon the
believer's experience, in some particulars with which I
was unacquainted: so that though I loved and valued
him, I considered him as a person misled by enthusiastical notions, and strenuously insisted that we should
never think alike till we met in heaven.

All along, in the progress of this inquiry, I grew more
and more concerned about my character. I saw myself
continually verging nearer and nearer to that scheme of
doctrine which the world calls Methodism; nor could I
help it without doing violence to my convictions. I had
indeed set out with the avowed, and I trust sincere,
resolution of seeking the truth as impartially as possible;
and of embracing it wherever I might find it, without
respect to interest, reputation, or any worldly consideration whatever. I had taken patiently, and sustained
comfortably, the loss of my opening prospect of preferment, I trust mainly from the supports of grace, and the
consciousness of having acted with integrity; yet I am
not sure but my deceitful heart might also derive some
support from a vain imagination that my character
would be no loser. Ambitious thirst after the praise of
men was much more my peculiar corruption, than
covetousness; and I had been in no ordinary degree
proud of my natural understanding. I had been accus-

tomed to hear the people called Methodists mentioned with contempt, as ignorant and deluded, as fools, and sometimes as madmen; and that with no small degree of complacency and self-preference, I too had despised them as weak enthusiasts. But I now began to be apprehensive that the tables were about to be turned upon me. If I professed and taught these doctrines, I must no longer be considered as a man of sober understanding, but as one of those persons whose heads, being naturally weak, had been turned by religious studies; and who, having fallen under the power of enthusiasm, had become no better than fools or madmen.

This was the sharpest trial I passed through; for I had not yet learned that, when we are reproached for the name of Christ, happy are we. Nor did I remember, with due consideration of the reasons assignable for so extraordinary a circumstance, that the apostles were 'fools for Christ's sake'; were deemed 'beside themselves'; and went 'through evil report and good report, as deceivers, and yet true'; that they were 'everywhere spoken against', as the men that 'turned the world upside down'; were treated as 'vain babblers', and 'accounted the filth of the world, and the offscouring of all things'. I did not consider that Jesus himself, the 'brightness of the Father's glory', the 'word and wisdom of God', who 'went about doing good', and 'spake as never man spake', was not only rejected, but despised as not worth hearing, as 'one that had a devil', as in league with the devil, as 'a blasphemer', 'a Samaritan', 'a madman', yea, 'a devil'. I read, indeed, but my understanding was not yet opened to understand such plain scriptures as these: 'If ye were of the world, the world would love his own: but because ye are not of the world, but I have chosen you out of the world, therefore

the world hateth you. Remember the word that I said
unto you, The servant is not greater than his lord. If
they have persecuted me, they will also persecute you',
(John 15.19, 20). 'The disciple is not above his master,
nor the servant above his lord. If they have called the
master of the house Beelzebub, how much more shall
they call them of his household?' (Matt. 10.24, 25).
'Blessed are ye, when men shall revile you, and persecute you, and shall say all manner of evil against you
falsely, for my sake. Rejoice, and be exceeding glad: for
great is your reward in heaven: for so persecuted they
the prophets which were before you' (Matt. 5.11, 12).
Not being aware of these consequences when my resolution was first formed, I was as one who had begun to
build without counting the cost; and was greatly disturbed when I saw the favourite idol of my proud heart,
my character, in such imminent danger.

It must be supposed that this apprehension would
make me cautious what doctrines I admitted into my
creed; and, unwilling to be convinced that those things
were true and important, the profession of which was
sure to bring infamy on my character; and that, even
after the fullest conviction, I should thus be rendered
very careful in what manner I preached them. In general,
however, though the conflict was sharp, I was enabled
to be faithful. The words, 'Necessity is laid upon me;
yea, woe is unto me if I preach not the gospel', were
commonly upon my mind when I penned my sermon,
and when I entered the pulpit: and though, when a bold
declaration of what I believed to be the truth, with an
offensive application of it to the consciences of my
hearers, drew opposition and calumny upon me, I have
secretly resolved to be more circumspect the next time;
yet, when that time came, my heart and conscience
being both engaged, I dared not to conceal one tittle of

what appeared to me to be true, and to promise usefulness. But while, with perturbation of mind, and with
many disquieting apprehensions, I declared the message with which I supposed myself to be intrusted; to
screen myself from the charge of Methodism, and to
soften the offence, I was frequently throwing out slighting expressions, and bringing the charge of enthusiasm
against those who preached such doctrines as I was not
yet convinced of. On the other hand, my concern about
my character quickened me very much in prayer, and
increased my diligence in searching the Scriptures, that
I might be sure I was not, at this expense, preaching
'cunningly devised fables', instead of feeding the souls
committed to my care with the unadulterated milk of
evangelical truth.

In this state of mind, which is more easily understood
by experience than description, I met with Mr Venn's
Essay on the Prophecy of Zacharias. Luke 1.67–79. I was no
stranger to the character he bore in the eyes of the world,
and did not begin to read this book with great alacrity
or expectation. However, the interesting subjects treated
of engaged my attention, and I read it with great
seriousness, and some degree of impartiality. I disap-
proved indeed of many things; but the truth and
importance of others brought conviction both to my
understanding and conscience: especially, I found a
word in season respecting my foolish and wicked shame
and attention to character, in inquiring after divine
truth, and in the performance of the important duties of
a gospel minister. These solemn words in particular
came home to my heart: 'If the spirit of the world, pride,
carelessness respecting the soul, and neglect of Christ,
be not hateful to God and destructive to men, the gospel
(with reverence I speak it) is an imposition. Do you
abhor that thought as blasphemy? Abhor as much a

fawning upon Christ from year to year in your closet,
calling him there your Lord and God, and then coming
out to consult the world how far they will allow you to
obey his plain commands, without saying you are a
Methodist. Cease rather to profess any allegiance to
Christ, than treat him, under professions of duty, with
such contempt. "I would," said he to the church of
Laodicea, "thou wert cold or hot"; but "because thou
are lukewarm, and neither cold nor hot, I will spue thee
out of my mouth." ' (Page 85.)

I should as easily be convinced that there was no Holy
Ghost, as that he was not present with my soul when I
read this passage, and the whole of what Mr Venn has
written upon the subject. It came to my heart with such
evidence, conviction, and demonstration, that it lifted
me up above the world, and produced that victory which
faith alone can give, and that liberty which uniformly
attends the presence of the Spirit of the Lord. I became
at once ashamed of my base ingratitude and foolish
fears, and was filled with such consolation and rejoicing,
even in the prospect of sacrificing my character, and
running the risk of infamy and contempt, as made me
entirely satisfied on that head: and, some few seasons of
unbelief excepted, I have never since been much
troubled about being called an enthusiast or a Methodist.

But while I was thus delivered from the dread of
unmerited reproaches, I continued as much as ever
afraid of real enthusiasm; nay, I became continually
more and more averse to everything which can justly
bear that name: so that the nearer I verged to what I had
ignorantly supposed to be enthusiastical, the more
apprehensive I was lest my earnestness in such interesting inquiries, and the warmth of my natural spirits,
thus occasionally increased, should put me off my guard,
and betray me into delusions and mistakes. From this

danger I could however obtain no security, but by keeping close to the study of the Word of God; and by being earnest and particular in praying to be preserved from error, and to be enabled to distinguish between the pure revelations of the Holy Spirit contained in Scripture, and the inventions of men, the imaginations of my own heart, or the delusions of the spirit of lies.

The doctrine of a Trinity of co-equal persons in the Unity of the Godhead had been hitherto no part of my creed. I had long been accustomed to despise this great mystery of godliness. I had first quarrelled with the Articles of the Established Church about this doctrine: I had been very decided and open in my declarations against it; and my unhumbled reason still retained many objections to it. But about June 1777, I began to be troubled with doubts about my own sentiments, and to suspect the truth of Dr Clarke's hypothesis. I had just read Mr Lindsey's *Apology* and *Sequel*. Before I saw these tracts, I had even ridiculed those who thought of confuting him on the orthodox scheme, and was not without thoughts of maintaining Dr Clarke's system against him. But, when I understood that he claimed Dr Clarke as a Socinian, I was extremely surprised, and, in consequence, was led again to a more serious and anxious consideration of the subject.

Yet, the more I studied, the more I was dissatisfied. Many things now first occurred to me as strong objections against my own sentiments; and, being thus perplexed, and unable to form a scheme for myself, I easily perceived that I was not qualified to dispute with another person. My pride and my convictions struggled hard for the victory: I was very unwilling to become a Trinitarian in the strict sense of the word, though, in my own sense, I had for some time pretended to be one; and yet the more I considered it, the more I was dissatisfied with all other systems. My esteem for Mr Newton was also now very much increased; and though I had hitherto concealed this part of my sentiments from him, yet I knew his to be very different. I was not indeed willing to be taught by him in other matters: yet, in this respect, finding his opinion the same which in all former ages of the church had been accounted orthodox, while that which I held had always been branded as heretical, my fears of a mistake were thus exceedingly increased. In this perplexity I applied to the Lord, and frequently besought him to lead me to a settled conclusion what was the truth in this important subject. After much meditation, together with a careful examination of all the scriptures which I then understood to relate to it, accompanied with earnest prayer for divine teaching, I was at length constrained to renounce, as utterly indefensible, all my former sentiments, and to accede to that doctrine which I had so long despised.

I saw, and I could no longer help seeing, that the offices and works, attributed in Scripture to the Son and to the Holy Spirit, are such as none but the infinite God could perform: that it is a contradiction to believe the real, and consequently infinite, satisfaction to divine justice made by the death of Christ, without believing him to be 'very God of very God'. Nor could the Holy Ghost give spiritual life, and dwell in the hearts of all believers at the same time, to adapt his work of convincing, enlightening, teaching, strengthening, sanctifying, and comforting to the several cases of every individual, were he not the omniscient, omnipresent, infinite God.

Being likewise certain, from reason as well as from Scripture, that there is not, and cannot be, more Gods than one, I was driven from my reasonings, and constrained to submit my understanding to divine revelation; and, allowing that the incomprehensible God alone can fully know the unsearchable mysteries of his own divine nature, and the manner of his own existence, to adopt the doctrine of a 'Trinity in Unity', among other reasons of still greater moment, in order to preserve consistency in my own scheme. It was, however, a considerable time before I was disentangled from my embarrassments on this subject.

Hitherto my prejudices against Mr Hervey, as a writer upon doctrinal subjects, had been very strong. I thought him a very pious man, and I had read with pleasure some parts of his *Meditations*; yet, looking on him as an enthusiast, I had no curiosity to read any other of his writings. But, about July 1777, I providentially met with his *Theron and Aspasio*; and opening the book, I was pleased with the first passage on which I cast my eye. This engaged me to read the whole with uncommon attention: nor did I, in twice perusing it, meet with any thing contrary to my own sentiments, without immediately beseeching the Lord to guide me to the truth. I trust the Lord heard and answered these prayers; for, though I could not but dissent from him (as I still do) in some few things; yet I was both instructed and convinced by his arguments and illustrations in everything relative to our fallen, guilty, lost, and helplessly miserable state by nature; and the way and manner in which the believer is accounted, and accepted as righteous, in the presence of a just, holy, and heart-searching, a faithful and unchangeable God: especially his animated description and application of the stag chase, cleared up this important matter to my mind, more than anything I had hitherto met with upon the subject.

I had now acceded to most of the doctrines which at present I believe and preach; except the doctrine of personal election, and those tenets which immediately depend on it and are connected with it. These were still foolishness to me: and, so late as August 1777, I told my friend Mr Newton that I was sure I never should be of his sentiments on that head. To this he answered, that if I never mentioned this subject, he never should, as we were now agreed in all he judged absolutely needful; but, that he had not the least doubt of my very shortly becoming a Calvinist, as I should presently discover my system of doctrine to be otherwise incomplete, and inconsistent with itself. Indeed, I had by this time so repeatedly discovered myself to be mistaken where I had been very confident, that I began to suspect myself in everything in which I entertained sentiments different from those with whom I conversed. This, however, did not influence me to take their opinions upon trust: but it disposed me more particularly and attentively to consider them; and in every perplexity to have recourse to the Lord to be preserved from error and guided to the truth.

About the same time also, I began to have more frequent applications made to me by persons under deep concern for their souls. My heart was much interested in this new employment, as I was greatly concerned to see their pressing anxieties, and to hear their doubts, difficulties, and objections, against themselves: and, being sincerely desirous to give them good instruction, and to lead them on to establishment and comfort, I felt my deficiency, and seemed to have no ground to go on, nor any counsel to give them, but what, instead of relieving them, led them into greater perplexity. In this case, I earnestly besought the Lord to teach me what word in season to speak unto them.

While I was thus circumstanced, I read Witsius' *Economy of the Covenants*, and observed what use he made of the doctrine of election for this very purpose.

This convinced me that the doctrine, if true, would afford that ground of encouragement which the people wanted. They had been awakened from ignorant formality, open ungodliness and vice, or entire carelessness about religion, to an earnest and anxious inquiry after salvation. They appeared truly penitent, and real believers, and heartily desirous of cleaving unto the Lord; and they wanted some security that they should not, through the deceitfulness of their hearts, their weakness, the entanglements of the world, and the temptations of Satan, fall back again into their former course of sin. This, if genuine, was the regenerating work of the Holy Spirit: and if wrought in consequence of the determinate purpose and foreknowledge of God respecting them, it would follow, from the entire and undeserved freeness of this first gift bestowed on them, when neither desiring nor seeking it, but while in a state of enmity and rebellion against God, and neglect of his service, and from his unchangeableness in his purpose, and faithfulness to his promises, that he would assuredly carry on and complete the good work of his grace, and keep them by his power, as in a castle, through faith unto salvation.

Having now discovered one use of this doctrine, which before I objected to as useless and pernicious, I was led to consider how the other objections which I had been accustomed to urge against it, might be answered. It is true, I now began to consider it as a mystery, not to be comprehended, nor yet too curiously to be searched into by man's natural reason, but humbly received by faith, just as far as it is plainly revealed in God's unerring Word. I was therefore constrained to leave many objections unanswered, or to resolve them into the incomprehensible nature of God, whose judgments and counsels are, as the great deep, unfathomable;

and into the sovereignty of God, who doeth what he
will with his own, and gives no account of any of his
matters, let who will presume to find fault; and into his
declarations, that his thoughts and ways are as far above
our thoughts and ways as the heavens are above the
earth. Here I left the matter, conscious, at length, that
such knowledge was too high for me; and that, if God
had said it, it was not my place to cavil against it.

I acknowledge this way of proceeding is not very
satisfactory to man's proud curiosity, who would be as
God, and know all that God knows, and who even dares
to dispute with him! And there are times when I can
hardly acquiesce in such a solution. But surely it is
highly becoming the dependent state and limited understanding of the creature, to submit the decision of all
such high points implicitly to the award of the infinitely
wise Creator. Indeed, the Christian religion expressly
requires it of us; for our Lord declared, that 'Except we
receive the kingdom of God' (not as disputing philosophers, but) 'as a little child, we shall in no wise enter
therein'. The day is coming when we shall be able to
answer all objections. Here 'we walk by faith', and see
in part, 'through a glass, darkly'; 'hereafter we shall see
face to face, and know even as we are known'.*

---

* The doctrine of personal election to eternal life, when properly
stated, lies open to no objection, which may not likewise, with equal
plausibility, be urged against the conduct of God in placing one nation
in a more favourable condition than another, especially as to religious
advantages; without the previous good or bad behaviour of either of
them, or any discernible reasons for the preference. In both cases we
may say, unmerited favour to one person or people, is no injustice to
others; and the infinitely wise God has many reasons for his deter-
minations, which we cannot discern, and which he deigns not to
make known to us.

If sinners deserve the punishment inflicted on them, it cannot be
unjust in the great Governor of the world to pre-determine their

condemnation to it. The contrariety to justice and goodness, if there be any, must certainly be found in the Lord's actual dealings with his creatures, and not in his pre-determinations thus to deal with them. It could not be inconsistent with any of the divine attributes, for the Lord from all eternity to decree to act consistently with all of them. The clamours excited against predestination, if carefully scrutinized, are generally found to be against the thing decreed, and not against the circumstance of its having been decreed from eternity. The sovereignty of God, when duly considered, appears to be nothing more than infinite perfection determining and accomplishing everything in the very best manner possible, and infallibly performing the counsels of everlasting knowledge and wisdom, justice, truth, and love, notwithstanding all the plans and designs of innumerable voluntary rational agents which might seem incompatible with them: nay, performing those counsels even by means of these voluntary agents, in perfect consistency with their free agency and accountableness, but in a manner which we are utterly incapable of comprehending.

We should scarcely object to this infinitely wise and holy sovereignty of God, however absolute, did we not, from consciousness of guilt and carnal enmity of heart, suspect that it might probably be found at variance with our happiness: and, I apprehend, should any man be fully persuaded that God had decreed his eternal happiness, however groundless that persuasion might be, he would find his aversion to the doctrine of election exceedingly abated by it. I have often observed that some persons, who declaim most vehemently against the Calvinistical doctrine of divine decrees, seem perfectly reconciled to predestination, when persuaded that God has eternally decreed the salvation of all men! On the other hand, no consciously impenitent sinner is cordially reconciled to the general declarations of Scripture, concerning the everlasting misery of all impenitent sinners, whatever he may think about personal election.

In fact, the grand difficulty in the whole of the divine conduct, equally embarrasses every system of Christianity, and every scheme of Deism, except men deny that God is the Creator and Governor of the world. For wickedness and misery actually exist and abound; the fact is undeniable. The Almighty God could have prevented this, and we should have thought that infinite love would have preserved the creation from all evils of every description. Yet, infinite wisdom saw good to permit them to enter, and amazingly to prevail! Till this difficulty be completely solved, let none object to truths plainly revealed in Scripture on account of similar difficulties. But let us remember, that our narrow capacities and scanty information do not qualify us to judge concerning what it becomes the infinite God to determine and to do; and let us adopt the language of the apostle on

THE DOCTRINES OF GRACE

Leaving therefore all difficulties of a metaphysical nature to be cleared up in that world of light and knowledge, I began to consider the abuses of this doctrine, which I had always looked upon as a very formidable objection against it. But I soon discovered, that though ungodly men who make profession of religion will turn the grace of God into licentiousness, yet we might so explain and guard these doctrines, that none could thus abuse them, without being conscious of it, and so detecting their own hypocrisy. It still indeed appeared probable to me, that the preaching of them might at first occasion some trouble of mind to a few well-disposed persons: but I considered that, by a cautious declaration, and contrasting them with the general promises of the gospel to all who believe, this might in a great measure be prevented. At the worst, a little personal conversation with such persons would seldom, if ever, fail to satisfy them, and enable them in general to derive encouragement from them: while the unsettling of the minds of such persons as are carelessly living in an unconverted state, is the great end of all our

---

this subject. 'O the depth of the riches both of the wisdom and knowledge of God! how unsearchable are his judgments, and his ways past finding out! For who hath known the mind of the Lord? or who hath been his counsellor? Or who hath first given to him, and it shall be recompensed unto him again? For of him, and through him, and to him, are all things: to whom be glory for ever. Amen.' (Rom. 11.33–36.)

As for the objections made to these doctrines, as inconsistent with free agency, accountableness, commands, invitations, calls to repentance, faith and holiness, and diligence in the use of means, they universally and altogether arise from misrepresentation and misapprehension of the subject. (See the author's *Sermon on Election and Final Perseverance, &c.* 5th Ed.).

preaching to them; and therefore we need not fear any bad effect of this doctrine in that respect.

The great question therefore was, Are these doctrines in the Bible, or not? Hitherto I had wilfully passed over or neglected, or endeavoured to put some other construction upon all those parts of Scripture which directly speak of them; but now I began to consider, meditate, and pray over them; and I soon found that I could not support my former interpretations. They would teach predestination, election, and final perseverance, in spite of all my twisting and expounding. It also occurred to me, that these doctrines, though now in disgrace, were universally believed and maintained by our venerable reformers; that they were admitted, at the beginning of the Reformation, into the Creeds, Catechisms, and Articles, of every one of the Protestant churches; that our Articles and Homilies expressly maintained them; and consequently, that a vast number of wise and soberminded men, who in their days were burning and shining lights, had upon mature deliberation agreed, not only that they were true, but that they ought to be admitted as useful, or even as necessary Articles of Faith, by every one who deemed himself called to take upon him the office of a Christian minister.

In the course of this inquiry, I perceived that my system was incomplete without them. I believed that men, by nature born in sin, the children of wrath, and by wicked works the enemies of God, being in themselves ungodly and without strength, were saved of free mercy and grace, without having done anything, more or less, to deserve it, through the Redeemer's righteousness and atonement, received by faith, the gift and operation of God; as born again, born of God, or new created unto good works, and to the divine image, by the power of the Holy Ghost.

It now, therefore, occurred to me to inquire, from what source these precious blessings, thus freely flowing through the channel of redemption to poor worthless sinners, could originally spring? And thus my mind was carried back from the consideration of the effects, to that of the cause; and from the promises made to fallen man, to the counsels and purposes of God which induced him to give those promises.

I was engaged in frequent meditations on the divine omniscience, unchangeableness, and eternity; and the end which the all-sufficient God had in view in all his works, even the manifestation of the glory of his own perfections; and perceived that redemption itself, as planned by God, to whom were 'known all his works from the beginning of the world', must be the result of his eternal purpose of displaying the glory of his mercy and grace, in harmonious consistency with his most awful justice and holiness; and thus manifesting the inexhaustible resources of his manifold wisdom, in glorifying at once all these attributes, which, considered as perfect, seem to created understanding irreconcilable with one another. I considered that, until the fall of man and his redemption had manifested the attribute of mercy to sinners, it had, as far as we can learn, been unexercised and undisplayed, and consequently unknown to any but God himself, from all eternity. Nor could he have the glory of it, but must have been considered as so perfect in justice and holiness, as to be incapable of mercy, had he not chosen some objects on whom to exercise it, and devised some method of displaying it in consistency with his other perfections.

Thus I perceived redemption to be the effect of a settled design, formed in God's eternal counsels, of manifesting himself to his reasonable creatures, complete and full-orbed in all conceivable perfections. But as all have transgressed the divine law, and as none are disposed of themselves to embrace his humbling and holy salvation, or even to inquire after it, so I was convinced that the merciful and gracious nature of God, the fountain of goodness, alone moved him to choose any of them as objects of his favourable regard; that his unconstrained will and pleasure are the only assignable causes of his choosing one rather than another; and that in fact the whole work was his own, his wisdom having devised the means; his love and all-sufficiency having, in the person, offices, and work of Christ, made all things ready; his providence directing absolutely to whom the word of invitation shall be sent; and his Holy Spirit alone inclining and enabling the soul to embrace it by faith.

Hence I concluded that God, who knoweth the end from the beginning, and is a Sovereign, and, when none have deserved any thing, may do as he will with his own, actually 'chose us' (even every individual believer) 'in Christ, before the foundation of the world, that we should be holy and without blame before him in love: having predestinated us unto the adoption of children by Jesus Christ to himself, according to the good pleasure of his will, to the praise of the glory of his grace, wherein he hath made us accepted in the Beloved'. (Eph: 1.4–6.)

In short, though my objections were many, my anxiety great, and my resistance long, yet by the evidence which, both from the Word of God and from my own meditation, crowded upon my mind, I was at length constrained to submit; and, God knoweth, with fear and trembling, to allow these formerly despised doctrines a place in my creed. Accordingly, about Christmas 1777, I began cautiously to establish the truth of them, and to make use of them for the consolation of poor, distressed and fearful believers. This was the only use I then knew of them, though I now see their influence on every part of evangelical truth.

However, I would observe that, though I assuredly believe these doctrines as far as here expressed (for I am not willing to trace them any higher, by reasonings or consequences, into the unrevealed things of God), and though I exceedingly need them in my view of religion, both for my own consolation, and security against the consequences of a deceitful heart, an ensnaring world, and a subtle tempter, as also for the due exercise of my pastoral office; yet I would not be understood to place the acknowledgment of them upon a level with the belief of the doctrines before spoken of. I can readily conceive the character of a humble, pious, spiritual Christian, who is either an utter stranger to the doctrines in question, or who, through misapprehension or fear of consequences, cannot receive them. But I own I find a difficulty in conceiving of a humble, pious, spiritual Christian, who is a stranger to his own utterly lost condition, to the deceitfulness and depravity of his heart, to the natural alienation of his affections from God, and to the defilements of his best duties, who trusts, either in whole or in part, allowedly, to anything for pardon and justification, except the blood and righteousness of a crucified Saviour, God manifested in the flesh; or who expects to be made meet for the inheritance of the saints in light in any other way than by being born again, created anew, converted and sanctified by the divine power of the Holy Ghost.

Some time in November 1777, I was, by a then unknown friend, furnished with a considerable number of books, written in general by the old divines, both of the Church of England, and of the dissenters. And, to my no small surprise, I found that those doctrines which are now deemed novel inventions, and are called

Methodistical, are in these books everywhere discoursed of as known and allowed truths; and that the system which, despising to be taught by men, and unacquainted with such authors, I had for near three years together been hammering out for myself, with no small labour and anxiety, was to be found ready made to my hand in every book I opened.

I do not wonder that the members of the Church of England are generally prejudiced against the writings of dissenters; for I have been so myself to an excessive degree. We imbibe this prejudice with the first rudiments of instruction, and are taught by our whole education to consider it as meritorious: though no doubt it is a prejudice of which every sincere inquirer after truth ought to be afraid, and every pretended inquirer ashamed; for how can we determine on which side truth lies, if we will not examine both sides? Indeed, it is well known to all those who are acquainted with the church histories of those times, that till the reign of James I there were no controversies between the Established Church and the Puritans concerning doctrine, both parties being in all matters of importance of the same sentiments. They contended only about discipline and ceremonies, till the introduction of Arminianism gave occasion to the Calvinists being denominated Doctrinal Puritans. To this period all our church writers were Calvinistical in doctrine; and even after that time, many might be mentioned, who were allowed friends to the Church of England, that opposed those innovations, and agreed in doctrine with everything above stated. Let it suffice, out of many, to recommend the works of Bishop Hall, especially his *Contemplations on the Life of Jesus*, a book not easily to be prized too highly; and Dr Reynolds' Works. To these, no true friend to the Church of England can reasonably object, and in general, I believe and teach nothing but what they plainly taught before me.

The outlines of my scheme of doctrine were now completed: but I had been so taken up with doctrinal inquiries, that I was still, in a great measure, a stranger to my own heart, and had little experience of the power of the truths I had embraced. The pride of reasoning, and the conceit of superior discernment, had all along accompanied me; and, though somewhat broken, had yet considerable influence. Hitherto, therefore, I had not thought of hearing any person preach; because I did not think any one, in the circle of my acquaintance, capable of giving me such information as I wanted. But, being at length convinced that Mr Newton had been right, and that I had been mistaken in the several particulars in which we had differed, it occurred to me that, having preached these doctrines so long, he must understand many things concerning them to which I was a stranger. Now, therefore, though not without much remaining prejudice, and not less in the character of a judge than of a scholar, I condescended to be his hearer, and occasionally to attend his preaching, and that of some other ministers. I soon perceived the benefit, for from time to time the secrets of my heart were discovered to me, far beyond what I had hitherto noticed; and I seldom returned from hearing a sermon without having conceived a meaner opinion of myself, without having attained to a further acquaintance with my deficiencies, weaknesses, corruptions, and wants; or without being supplied with fresh matter for prayer, and directed to greater watchfulness. I likewise learned the use of experience in preaching, and was convinced that the readiest way to reach the hearts and consciences of others was to speak from my own. In short, I gradually saw more and more my need of instruction, and was at length brought to consider myself as a very novice in religious matters. Thus I began experimentally to perceive our Lord's meaning when he says, 'Except ye receive the kingdom of God as a little child, ye shall in no wise enter therein.' For though my proud heart is continually rebelling, and would fain build up again the former Babel of self-conceit, yet I trust I have from this time, in my settled judgment, aimed and prayed to be enabled to consider myself as a little child, who ought simply to sit at the Master's feet, to hear his words with profound submission, and wait his teaching with earnest desire and patient attention. From this time I have been enabled to consider those persons, in whom knowledge has been ripened by years, experience, and observation, as fathers and instructors, to take pleasure in their company, to value their counsels, and with pleasure to attend their ministry.

Thus, I trust, the old building which I had purposed to repair, was pulled down to the ground, and the foundation of the new building of God laid aright. 'Old things passed away; behold, all things were become new.' 'What things were gain to me, those I have counted loss for Christ.' My boasted reason I have discovered to be a blind guide, until humbled, enlightened, and sanctified by the Spirit of God; my former wisdom, foolishness; and that when I thought I knew much, I knew nothing as I ought to know. Since this period, everything I have experienced, heard, or read, and everything I observe around me, confirms and establishes me in the assured belief of those truths which I have received; nor do I in general any more doubt whether they be from God, than I doubt whether the sun shines when I see its light and am warmed with its refreshing beams. I see the powerful effects of them continually among those to whom I preach; I experience the power of them daily in my own soul; and, while by meditating on and 'glorying in the cross of Christ, I find the world crucified unto me, and I unto the world', by preaching Jesus Christ and him crucified, I see notoriously immoral persons, taught by the saving grace of God, to 'deny ungodliness and worldly lusts, and to live soberly, righteously, and godly in this present world', being examples to such as before they were a scandal to.

And now, by this change, the consequences of which I so much dreaded, what have I lost, even in respect of this present world? Indeed, I have lost some degree of favour, and I escape not pity, censure, scorn, and opposition: but the Lord is introducing me to a new and far more desirable acquaintance, even to that of those whom the Holy Spirit has denominated the excellent of the earth; nay, the Lord the Spirit condescends to be my Comforter. In general, I enjoy an established peace of conscience, through the blood of sprinkling, and continual application to the heavenly Advocate; with a sweet content, and that peace of conscience which 'passeth all understanding', in 'casting all my cares upon him who careth for me': and I am not left utterly without experience of that 'joy which is unspeakable and full of glory'. These the world could not give me, were I in favour with it; of these it cannot deprive me by its frowns. My desire, henceforth, God knows, is to live to his glory, and by my whole conduct and conversation 'to adorn the doctrine of God my Saviour', and 'to show forth his praises, who hath called me out of darkness into his marvellous light'; to be in some way or other useful to his believing people, and to invite poor sinners, who are 'walking in a vain show, and disquieting themselves in vain', to 'taste and see how gracious the Lord is, and how blessed they are who put their trust in him'.

'Now would I tell to sinners round
What a dear Saviour I have found,
Would point to his redeeming blood,
And cry, Behold the way to God!'

Thus has the Lord led me, a poor blind sinner, in a way that I knew not. 'He has made darkness light before me, crooked things straight', and hard things easy, and has brought me to a place of which I little thought when I set out; and having done these things for me, I believe, yea, I am undoubtedly sure, he will never leave me nor forsake me. To him be the glory of his undeserved and long-resisted grace! To me be the shame, not only of all my other sins, but also of my proud and perverse opposition to his purposes of love towards me! But all this was permitted, that my high spirit and stout heart being at length humbled and subdued, 'I might remember, and be confounded, and never open my mouth any more, because of my shame, now that the Lord is pacified to me for all that I have done'.

And now, as in the presence of the heart-searching Judge, I have given, without one wilful misrepresentation, addition, or material omission, a history of the great things God has done for my soul; or if that suit not the reader's view of it, a history of that change which has recently taken place in my religious sentiments and conduct, to the surprise of some, and perhaps the displeasure of others, among my former friends. The doctrines I have embraced are indeed charged with being destructive of moral practice, and tending to licentiousness; but though I know that my best righteousnesses are as filthy rags, yet I trust I may return thanks to God, that by his grace he has so upheld me since this change took place, that I have not been permitted to disgrace the cause in which I have embarked by any immoral conduct. 'My rejoicing,' in this respect, 'is this, that in simplicity and godly sincerity, not with fleshly wisdom, but by the grace of God, I have my conversation in the world.' I can confidently avow that the belief of these doctrines has a quite contrary effect upon me. I most earnestly desire, aim, endeavour, and pray to be enabled to love God, and keep his commandments, 'without partiality, and without hypocrisy'; and so to demean myself as 'by well-doing to put to silence the ignorance of foolish men'. That I fall so very far short in everything is not the effect of my new doctrines, but of my old depraved nature and deceitful heart. 'Create in me a clean heart, O God, and renew a right spirit within me!'

PART THREE

Observations on the Preceding Narrative

My design in writing this account of myself, and my religious inquiries and change of sentiments, was this: I consider myself as a singular instance of a very unlikely person, in an uncommon manner, being led on from one thing to another, to embrace a system of doctrine which he once heartily despised. As I assuredly believe that this change has been effected under the guidance and teaching of the Holy Spirit, so I hoped that a circumstantial relation of it might be an encouragement and comfort to those who know and love the Lord, and from them levy a tribute of gratitude and praise to our gracious God: and that it also might be instrumental, by the convincing Spirit, to awaken others to a serious review of their religious sentiments; to put them upon the same earnest inquiry after the truth as it is in Jesus; and to influence them to the diligent use of the same blessed means, in which the Lord directed me to be found. I would therefore now offer a few observations on the preceding narrative: and may the Lord guide both the writer, and every reader of these pages, to the saving knowledge of the truth, and into the ways of peace and righteousness.

I. SCOTT'S EARLY RELIGIOUS OPINIONS

It must be evident to every unprejudiced reader of this narrative that, at the time this change commenced, I was, humanly speaking, a most unlikely person to embrace the system of doctrine above stated. This will appear from the following considerations:

(1) My religious opinions had been for many years directly contrary to it. Being always of a reflecting turn of mind, I entertained exceedingly high notions of the powers of human reason; and I had, upon reasoning principles, embraced a system of religion which both soothed my conscience and flattered my self-conceit. After some trivial alterations, I seemed to myself, upon mature deliberation, to have come to a settled determination, and had bestowed considerable pains in making myself acquainted with those arguments and interpretations of Scripture by which that system is usually defended. I had also ranked together many of those plausible objections and high charges which are commonly brought by reasoning men against the doctrines and characters of the Calvinists. But I was in a great measure a stranger to what the Calvinists could say for themselves, because I thought the matter too plain to bear an argument, and therefore did not think their answers worth reading. In short, very few have been recovered from that abyss of error (for so I must call it) into which I had been permitted to sink. Full of confidence in my cause, and in the arguments with which I was prepared to support it, I was eager to engage in controversy with the Calvinists, and entertained the most sanguine hopes of victory. In this confidence I frequently harangued against them from the pulpit, and spared not to charge upon them consequences both absurd and shocking. Yet, after much, very much, anxious diligent inquiry, I have embraced, as the sacred truths of God's unerring Word, every doctrine of this despised system!

(2) My natural spirit and temper were very unfavourable to such a change. Few persons have ever been more

self-sufficient and positive in their opinions than I was. Fond to excess of entering into argument, I never failed on these occasions to betray this peculiarity of my character. I seldom acknowledged or suspected myself mistaken; and scarcely ever dropped an argument, till either my reasonings or obstinacy had silenced my opponent. A certain person once said of me, that I was like a stone rolling down a hill, which could neither be stopped nor turned. This witness was true, but those things which are impossible with man, are easy with God. I am evidently both stopped and turned. Man, I am persuaded, could not have done it. But this has God wrought, and I am not more a wonder to others than to myself. Indeed, I carried the same obstinate, positive temper into my religious inquiries; for I never gave up one tittle of my sentiments till I could defend it no longer, nor ever submitted to conviction till I could no longer resist. The strong man armed with my natural pride and obstinacy, with my vain imaginations and reasonings and high thoughts, had built himself many strongholds, and kept his castle in my heart; and when one stronger than he came against him he stood a long siege: till, being by superior force driven from one to another, and all his armour in which he trusted being at length taken from him, he was constrained to recede. So that the Lord having made me willing in the day of his power, I was forced to confess, 'O Lord, thou art stronger than I, and hast prevailed.'

(3) My situation in life rendered such a change improbable. I had an increasing family, no private fortune, a narrow precarious income, and no expectations, except from such friends as my conduct might procure or continue to me. I had unexpectedly contracted an acquaintance with some of those whose favour goes a great way towards a man's advancement in life; nor

was I insensible to the advantages to be hoped for from cultivating by a compliant behaviour their kind and friendly regard to me. At the same time, I was no stranger to the opinion which the world entertains of those who preach these disreputable doctrines, and could not but conclude that embracing them would probably deprive me of these prospects of preferment. But, as the result of diligent inquiry, I was assuredly convinced that it was my indispensable duty to profess and preach them, and that by so doing alone, I could ensure to myself the favour of a better Friend than any here below. And thus, while fully aware all along how unfavourable, according to human probability, it would prove to my worldly interests, I at length deliberately embraced them.

(4) My regard to character was no trifling security against such a change of sentiment. I was ambitiously and excessively fond of that honour which comes from man; and considered the desire of praise as allowable, nay, laudable. By this motive was I urged on to a very diligent prosecution of my studies, even beyond what natural inclination led me to; and my whole conduct was influenced by, my whole conversation was tinctured with, this vainglorious aim. On the other hand, with approbation and self-complacency, I had been accustomed to hear the most contemptuous and opprobrious epithets liberally bestowed on those persons to whom I have now joined myself. And all along, as I verged nearer and nearer to Methodism, I was painfully sensible that I was drawing upon myself the same mortifying distinctions. I have been a vainglorious candidate for human applause; but I renounce such pretensions, and willingly submit to be considered by the world under the mortifying character of a half-witted, crack-brained enthusiast. These epithets I am sensible are now

bestowed upon me behind my back, nay, very often to my face. I bless God, however, this does not move me; but I can heartily thank him, that I am counted worthy to suffer shame for his sake. But when I saw the trial approaching, it appeared very formidable; and I can truly affirm, that nothing but the fullest conviction that the cause in which I was embarking was the cause of God – nothing, but not daring to act contrary to the plain dictates of my conscience, could have influenced me to make this sacrifice of my character, and bring upon myself so much scorn and contempt.

(5) To reason with our despisers upon their own principles: if I am now fallen into enthusiasm, mistake, and strong delusion, I certainly was, when I first set out in this inquiry, a very unlikely person so to do. My leading resolve was to search for the truth diligently, and to embrace it wherever I found it, and whatever it might cost. No sooner had I begun the inquiry, than I was called upon to give proof of the sincerity of this resolution; and from a principle of conscience, though a mistaken one, I renounced my prospect of an immediate preferment; and it would be uncandid to question my sincerity after it had been thus evidenced. Since that time I have also deliberately sacrificed my character, and hazarded the loss of all my former friends. Giving these proofs of integrity, I set off in dependence on those plain promises which I have mentioned. I have sought this desired knowledge of the truth, chiefly in reading the Holy Scriptures, and by prayer for the promised teaching of the Holy Ghost, in the manner which has been related; and I am now led to conclusions diametrically opposite to what I expected!

Now, lay all these things together, and attentively consider them, and then let your own consciences determine how far it is probable, that a person, in this

manner seeking for the truth, should be given over to a
strong delusion to believe a pernicious lie. 'If a son shall
ask bread of any of you that is a father, will he give him
a stone? or if he ask a fish, will he for a fish give him a
serpent? or if he shall ask an egg, will he give him a
scorpion? If ye, then, being evil, know how to give good
gifts unto your children, how much more shall your
heavenly Father give the Holy Spirit to them that ask
him?' Can any man suppose, that after such repeated
and continued pleading of the express promises of the
Lord to this effect, in earnest prayer, according to his
appointment, I should be delivered up to the teaching
of the father of lies? Can any one make this conclusion
without an evident insinuation that God has broken his
promises?

In short, you may make a jest of the narrative; you
may throw by the book without giving any attention to
an argument of this kind; you may say, what you never
can prove, that it is all a contrived story; or you may
argue, that these promises, though contained in the
Bible, are not to be depended on by us, which is to give
up the Scriptures to be scoffed at by infidels and atheists,
and to render them useless to the humble anxious
inquirer after truth and salvation. But by no other
means, I am assured, can you account for this single
circumstance, without allowing that the substance of
those doctrines which I have now embraced is indeed
contained in the Word of God; that they comprise the
truth as it is in Jesus, and are not corrupted with any
such delusion as can hazard the salvation of my soul, or
the souls of those who by my ministry receive them.

On this supposition all difficulties vanish. The Lord
had given me a sincere desire to know the saving
doctrine of the gospel; and though I was exceedingly
ignorant, obstinate, and prejudiced, yet this desire

having, according to his direction, led me to the Word
of God, and influenced me to seek his teaching by
prayer, he was faithful to his own promises, and it was
an example of his own words, 'Every one that asketh
receiveth, and he that seeketh findeth'. My evident
sincerity in seeking the truth was sufficient to convince
any person, conversant and experienced in the things of
God, that, as my friend foretold, thither would all my
inquiries lead me; in that would they all finally centre.
And could I be assured, beloved reader, whoever thou
art, that thou wast as sincerely desirous to know the
truth as I then was, and as heartily resolved to embrace
it wherever thou mightest find it, and whatever it should
cost thee; had I also assurance that, in a believing
dependence on these promises, thou wast diligently,
and from day to day, in the study of the Word of God
and prayer, seeking the accomplishment of them; I
would as confidently foretell, that, as to those things
which I now regard as essential to salvation, and, if thou
hast the souls of others committed to thee, as to what is
needful for thy usefulness in the ministry, thou wouldest
be brought in time to these same conclusions, whatever
thy present religious sentiments may be. May the Lord
give thee true sincerity, and incline thine heart to try
the experiment!

I am aware that many will object to what I have argued
on this head, as being too confident; and as what is
urged by men of contrary religious sentiments, each in
behalf of his own system: and, as I could not leave any
material and plausible objection in force against what I
have advanced, I hope the reader will excuse my
obviating this beforehand. I would therefore entreat
those who object to the confidence with which this
argument is brought forward, impartially and carefully
to consider the limitations with which on every hand it

is guarded; and then to inquire, whether in any other way than that which has been mentioned, they can account for the fact. That is, supposing this narrative true (for which the appeal is to the heart-searching God) and supposing the promises mentioned to be proposed to us, that we may embrace them, depend on them, and plead them in prayer, considering the glory of the divine veracity as concerned in their accomplishment to every believer; let them try whether they can possibly evade one of these conclusions: either God has failed of his promise; or he has, in the main, and as far as is expressed, led the author by his Holy Spirit to the knowledge and belief of the truth.

As to the confidence of men of opposite sentiments, I observe, that many, who speak in high terms concerning sincerity and candour, will without hesitation condemn as enthusiastical such reliance on the promises, and this way of searching for truth; and it is plain they do not seek truth in that manner which they condemn in others. Many others perhaps slightly mention these matters, but they will not endure to be closely questioned; for, being conscious that they have not sought the truth in this manner, they evade such discourse as personal. Again, the writings of many professed inquirers after truth evidently show that they expect to find it, not by 'trusting in the Lord with all their heart', or seeking it from the Scriptures, and by earnest prayer for the teaching of the Holy Spirit, but by 'leaning to their own understanding'; resting the argument on philosophical reasonings, and the authority of this or that renowned name; and supporting their conclusions by bold and perplexing criticisms and interpretations of Scripture.

Hence so many daring appeals from revelation to reason and philosophy! hence such and so many objec-

tions, brought against doctrines plainly revealed in
God's Word, if language has any determinate meaning!
and so many consequences charged upon these doctrines, with a design to invalidate their divine authority;
as if the appearance of unreasonableness, imposed by
every disingenuous art, were sufficient to prove the
plainest revelation of God's Holy Spirit a falsehood!
Hence such liberty in interpretation and criticism of the
Word of God, as the learned would never endure in
interpreting or criticising Virgil or Horace! These things
prove that such persons are strangers to that earnest,
hearty, sincere desire to know the truth, which brings
the inquirer to an humble willingness to be taught of
God, and, in submission of understanding, to seek
wisdom from his Word and Spirit. It is indeed most
evident, that many who profess to be influenced by this
sincere desire to know the truth are not troubled with
suspicions that they are, or can be wrong. They have
made up their minds before they begin the inquiry. You
will not find them willing to make the least concession,
but, in the management of the controversy, resolved to
vindicate and contend for every tittle; and where arguments fail, to make use of the other arts of controversy,
with which skill in the management of their weapons,
and anger against their opponents, can supply them.
Where a cause is thus maintained, you may easily know
that there is none of that earnest desire of learning the
truth, that anxious fear of mistaking it, that self-diffid-
ence, and those doubts concerning the sentiments held
at present, which constitute the godly sincerity that
leads the inquirer to the Word and Spirit of God for
direction and teaching.

These things taken together, will, on scriptural
grounds, cut off many confident pretenders to sincerity
from their claims, as entirely as they exclude Annas and

Caiaphas, and the chief priests, scribes, and Pharisees, from being sincere inquirers into the truth of the Old Testament, when in support of their authority and reputation, and influenced by pride and anger, they, under colour of their law, put to death 'Him of whom Moses and the prophets did write, even Jesus of Nazareth, the Son of God'. And as to men of another spirit, who appear sincere, humble, and willing to be taught of God in their inquiry after truth, but do not entirely agree with what has been laid down, I would only wish them to observe the distinction established between some and others of these doctrines. Such persons do not, I dare say, materially differ from that which has been mentioned as necessary to salvation: as, therefore, I allow them to have been in the main taught of God, so I only require the same allowance. Let it be supposed that the same God, who, according to his promise, has led both, as far as is needful to salvation, in the same way, has in other things left us to differ, for the mutual exercise of candour and forbearance, till that time when we shall know even as we are known.

2: CHANGE IN SENTIMENTS VERY GRADUAL

I would observe, that this change in my sentiments took place very gradually.

When any person suddenly changes his religious opinions for others very different from them, it is no inconsiderable evidence of a changeable and fickle disposition. It gives cause to suspect that he was not well established in his former sentiments; and that he had taken them upon trust, and was a stranger to the arguments by which they might be defended, and to the objections which might be urged against them. If worldly interest, reputation, or conveniency seem to favour the change, there is room for a presumption, that these had an undue influence upon him. If not, it may be insinuated that he was deluded with specious appearances; that he did not allow himself time to weigh the arguments on each side; and that he had only changed one set of notions for another, without having duly considered either of them.

Such objections may reasonably be made, and the consequences of precipitate changes too often justify them. But though I was always, and still am, of a headlong, impetuous spirit in other things, and when once I have purposed, can have no rest from incessant agitation of mind, till I have accomplished my design, yet in this particular I acted in direct opposition to my natural temper. Indeed, at first I did in some instances too much betray my impetuosity. But at that time I acted not in the character of an inquirer, but in full confidence that I was pleading the cause of truth, and had no more thought of becoming what the world calls a Methodist, than of turning Mohammedan. But after that first hurry was over, though commonly in earnest, and sometimes in considerable perturbation of mind, I was outwardly calm and satisfied, being generally enabled to believe that, if I were in anything at present mistaken, I should some time be guided to the truth. My determination to set about this inquiry proceeded not so much from anxious fears about my own soul, as from a deep sense impressed upon my heart of the importance of my ministry, the worth of the souls committed to my charge, and the awful account to be given of them; and as I all along bestowed some pains in instructing my people in what I believed to be the truth, I was preserved from any discomposing fears or undue disquietude of mind. I sat down very coolly to search for the truth. I proceeded very gradually, and with extreme caution. I took no one opinion upon trust. I gave up none of my sentiments, until the arguments by which I learned to defend them were satisfactorily answered; nor did I admit any new articles into my creed, till either every objection was obviated, or I was pressed on the other hand with such as were still more unanswerable.

Much, very much prayer and meditation preceded every change of sentiment; and I was nearly three years, from the beginning of my inquiry, before I came to a determination what was truth. So long, deliberately, and step by step, I examined the premises, before I finally proceeded to draw my conclusion. I perceive much cause to be ashamed of my unteachable temper; for with such opportunities as were afforded me, if I had improved them, I might have attained to the knowledge and belief of the same truths in much less time. But the Lord, I trust, led me in this way, and left me thus far to my own natural pride of heart, that it might more evidently appear that I received not my doctrines from man, but that indeed, in the first instance, I learned them from the Word and Spirit of God.

3: CHANGE IN VIEWS NOT DUE TO OTHER EVANGELICALS

I would observe that I changed my religious views without any teaching from the persons to whose sentiments I have now acceded. For a considerable time after the commencement of my inquiries, I would not so much as read what they had to urge in their own behalf. I entered indeed into a correspondence with Mr Newton. My intention, however, was not to learn from him, but to dispute with him; and when he waived controversy, I dropped the correspondence, and utterly neglected his letters. From that time I avoided his company, and all the while I declined hearing him preach. I would not be understood to insinuate that Mr Newton has not been useful to me: he has been, and continues to be, eminently so; and I continually see great cause to bless God for giving me such a friend, to be so near at hand on all occasions. But this I assuredly believe, that had I never seen him, at least from the time that his example had put me upon considering my conduct, I should have arrived at the same views of evangelical truth which I now have. His usefulness to me has all along been in those matters in which we were in some measure agreed, not in those in which we differed; for as to these, my proud heart scorned to have him for a teacher.

At the same time, though I had the offer of several books written by dissenters and Methodists, I declined it; and did not, for nearly two years, peruse any of them with sufficient attention to recollect any thing of consequence which they contained. I say not this as slighting these books; for justice requires me to acknowledge, that many, which then I ignorantly despised, contained as solid, judicious, and excellent divinity as has been penned since the days of the apostles. But I did not get my system from them; for that was nearly complete before I was prevailed upon to read them. My studies, besides the Bible, were chiefly confined to authors of allowed reputation in the Church of England, several of which I have mentioned. When they differed from one another (as certainly Tillotson and Hooker, Jortin and Beveridge, Bull and Hall differ very much indeed), I endeavoured to judge for myself, comparing all of them with the Word of God, and with the Articles, Homilies, and Liturgy of the Church of England. And from such authors, thus compared, as far as the writings of uninspired men have been instrumental to this change, I have received the greatest part of my present opinions.

But let it be observed, that the further these streams

are traced upward towards the fountain of the blessed
Reformation, the purer they flow, according to my
present judgment. And it may easily and undeniably be
proved, that there is nothing material preached by many
regular clergymen of the Establishment, under the scandal of Methodistical, which was not expressly taught by
those excellent persons, who, having laid the foundation
of our Church, gave their bodies to be burned in
confirmation of their doctrine. It is greatly to be wished
that their lives and discourses, living and dying, and
their remaining writings, were more generally known
among us, and did not remain locked up from the world
in large folios in the learned languages, and in books
out of print, or exceedingly scarce. In consequence of
this, the members of our national Church are in general
utterly ignorant of its standard doctrines, and ignorantly
brand those as Methodists and enthusiasts, who preach
zealously the very doctrines of the first Reformers.

4: STUDY OF THE SCRIPTURES PRODUCED THE CHANGE

I would observe the great influence which the study
of the Scriptures had in producing this change.

We are all too apt, without careful examination, to
take things for granted, especially in respect of religion.
We often collect our scheme of divinity from other
authors, or from our own reasonings and imaginations;
and only seek for a few detached texts which appear to
countenance our preconceived opinions; neglecting, or
very slightly considering, such parts of the Word of God
as seem incapable of being made use of to our purpose.
We are likewise too prone, in availing ourselves of the
labours of critics and expositors, to resign up ourselves
implicitly to their guidance, and to imagine that we
have proof enough of our doctrines, if we can produce

the sanction of some great name that has espoused and maintained them, without carefully examining whether they be right or wrong. But this is to pay that deference to the human interpretation, which is only due to the divine book commented on. We ministers, especially, though at ordination we solemnly promise to turn all our studies, as much as may be, into this channel, are very apt to suffer our time and thoughts to be engrossed with such studies and employments as are foreign to our profession, and interfere with it, and which leave at most but a secondary attention for the study of the Word of God. And who can deny, that many do not bestow so much pains in meditating upon the Bible, and in comparing spiritual things with spiritual, or one part of Scripture with another, and every part with what they experience in their own hearts, and what they hear and see in the world around them, as they do about matters of far less consequence? So that probably, should they at any time sit down to diligent examination of the whole Word of God, they would find it a very different book than they expected. Thus at least it has been with me, and possibly it may be so with many others.

The Word of God informs us that true wisdom, the saving, practical, and experimental knowledge of Divine things, is not to be acquired without earnest and diligent seeking. 'My son, if thou wilt receive my words, and hide my commandments with thee, so that thou incline thine ear unto wisdom, and apply thine heart to understanding; yea, if thou criest after knowledge, and liftest up thy voice for understanding; if thou seekest her as silver, and searchest for her as for hid treasures; then shalt thou understand the fear of the Lord, and find the knowledge of God' (Prov. 2. 1–5). If then our wisdom has been acquired without any of that eagerness and painful diligence with which the covetous man desires and seeks for his riches, it is a shrewd conjecture that it is not of the genuine sort. Once I had in my own esteem a sort of wisdom, which seemed to offer itself to me spontaneously, and to be found with little seeking. But now I am persuaded it was a mere counterfeit, a fair-seeming pernicious foolishness.

That which I now esteem to be true wisdom, if I could but attain to it, is not to be acquired in so easy a manner. When I first began to desire and seek this wisdom, I set out with the assurance that it was to be found in the Holy Scriptures, and nowhere else; they alone being able to make us wise unto salvation. I therefore considered myself engaged to make them my study: and as the whole was 'given by inspiration from God', and was all declared to be profitable, according to the various ends which the Holy Spirit designed in it, I made the whole my study. Thus I learned to look upon the Bible as my book of instructions, given me along with the ministerial office by my Lord and Master, that from thence I might deduce all my doctrines, instructions and admonitions, warnings, examples, encouragements, rules of duty, and motives to duty. I also considered it to be the believer's charter of privileges, containing exceedingly great and precious promises, and the whole of that which God saw fit to reveal concerning those unspeakable and inconceivable good things which he has of his infinite mercy prepared for them that love him. In order therefore faithfully to declare my message from the Lord Almighty to the souls of men, I found it indispensably needful to be well acquainted with every part, and to take the Word of God, myself, as well as propose it to others, as 'the lantern of my feet, and the light of my paths'; not only attending to the letter but also to the true meaning, the mind of the Spirit of God in it. This I found to be a work that required much time, great diligence, mature consideration, and an unbiassed, unprejudiced mind.

With this view of the matter partly obtained, and continually more and more unfolding itself, I studied the Word of God; and have now for nearly four years thus employed a very considerable part of my time, neither rejecting, nor yet greatly depending on, the assistance of interpreters. I sincerely desired to know the truth, and for that end I read the Scriptures, 'not as the word of man, but as the Word of God'. And though there have been seasons of remissness, when other employments and studies too much interfered with this main business; and though at first I was very far from an unbiassed mind, being blindly and obstinately prejudiced against those doctrines which I now believe to be the true gospel of Jesus Christ; yet in that space, I have read the Bible many times over, in every part with the strictest attention of which I have been capable. There are very few passages which relate to doctrine, that I have not repeatedly and diligently examined, comparing one with another with all the care and consideration I could. I seldom ever ceased meditating on any portion of Scripture until I had attained to some satisfying conclusion concerning its true meaning and its agreement with other scriptures. I may truly say, I have filled reams of paper with religious discussions, with sermons, expositions, and letters; in all which I ransacked the Bible, to bring as much scriptural evidence for my direction as possible. For these last two years I have scarcely opened a book except upon religious subjects, and from morning till night, nearly every day, all this while, my thoughts incessantly have been employed in meditation upon the great truths of the gospel. Every difficulty and objection (and difficulties and objections, both from my own meditations and in the course of my reading, continually crowded upon my mind) sent me to the Word of God, and increased my care and attention in examining and weighing every text of Scripture respecting the point in question, before I exchanged my old opinion for a new one.

Thus, I may truly say, I have sought in the Word of God (that field in which alone this precious treasure lies hid) 'for wisdom', for the saving knowledge of divine things, 'as for silver, and searched for her as for hid treasure'. And though I am sensible that my knowledge is still comparatively superficial, the knowledge of a child, of a novice in the school of Christ; yet, I trust that, as far as relates to the leading truths of the gospel, according to the promise, I am brought 'to understand the fear of the Lord, and have found the knowledge of God'.

Permit me now, beloved reader, to put thee in remembrance, that until thou hast, with some good measure of this diligence, studied the whole Word of God, thou runnest very great hazards in passing judgment upon men and doctrines. Be cautious what thou doest; let these men quite alone, until thou hast imitated the conduct of the noble Bereans, and thoroughly, and with unbiassed mind, examined and meditated upon the whole Word of God, to see whether the things they believe and teach be so or not; lest otherwise it should come to pass (as probably it will), that, in opposing and condemning them, thou shouldst be found to fight against God. Oh! that the Lord would hear and grant my request, and by his Holy Spirit powerfully incline the hearts of all who read these sheets, according to their leisure, station in life, obligations and opportunities, thus attentively to read their Bibles; not as the word of man, but as the Word of God himself, speaking from heaven unto them, and concerning the everlasting interests of their precious and immortal souls! Be the adviser what he will, despised and deserving to be despised, the advice is undoubtedly good: advice he will have no occasion to repent having thus given, at the solemn hour of death and the awful day of judgment; advice which, at those approaching seasons, none will repent having followed, though it should divert them from more amusing, and at this day more reputable studies, or engross that time which they have been accustomed to devote to more pleasurable and fashionable employments, but which, neglected, will be an additional sting in every conscience through all the countless ages of eternity.

And, oh! that they to whom the chief Shepherd has committed the care of precious souls, and at whose hands he will assuredly require every one that perishes through their default, would take in good part this expression of the very affectionate desire of my soul, both in behalf of them and of their flocks, in dropping these hints concerning their peculiar obligations to devote much of their time to the attentive unbiassed study of the Word of God, that infinitely best, but often least studied of all books! What avails it, that the ministers of the everlasting gospel should be learned, classical scholars, profound philosophers, metaphysicians, and mathematicians, expert logicians, or adorned with the knowledge of the politer sciences, if they are unacquainted, or but superficially acquainted with the sacred Scriptures? These other branches of literature may amuse and entertain them, may procure them preferment, reputation, respect, and favour; but the knowledge of the Bible alone can enable them, in such a manner to 'take heed to themselves, and to their doctrine', as shall issue in the everlasting salvation of their own souls and the souls committed to their care.

Far be it from me to presume to lay down my opinions as the standard of doctrine, or a rule for the faith and preaching of my brethren in the sacred ministry; but the more obscure I am, the less objection can there reasonably be against my hinting to them that, if any one should find this subject manifest itself to his conscience and make him sensible, that verily he hath been faulty in attending to other employments and studying other books more than the Word of God; then, possibly, he may be mistaken in his sentiments concerning the doctrines of the gospel, and, being mistaken himself, may be misleading others, to the endangering of their immortal souls: for he cannot be certain but that, should he employ some years in this single study (which its importance well deserves), he may find the Bible a very different book than he expected.

5: INFLUENCE OF PRAYER IN EFFECTING THE CHANGE

I would observe the influence which prayer appears to have had in effecting this change.

I am aware that the world, though called Christian, is come to such a pass, that the very mention of this subject in many companies is accounted ill manners, or even received with ridicule; and that being known to maintain a constant communion with God, by prayer and supplication with thanksgiving, is alone sufficient to denominate any person a Methodist. It is, however, most certain, that the Word of God is full of precepts, instructions, exhortations, invitations, promises, and examples to this effect. He never read his Bible, who knows not this. Nor can any man, under any pretence whatever, make a jest of this great duty and privilege of a believer, without pouring contempt upon the Holy Scriptures, and insulting the brightest characters there

proposed to us as examples, not excepting the Lord
Jesus himself.

Let men, therefore, under the profession of Christianity, be as irreligious and profane as they please, I shall
not be ashamed to speak upon so unfashionable a topic:
for if the Word of God be true, he never knew any thing
as he ought to know, never believed, never repented,
never performed one duty aright in his life, who has not
sought all his wisdom, knowledge, faith, repentance,
and sufficiency for obedience, from God, by fervent,
instant, persevering prayer. Time was, even since I had
souls committed to my care, that I lived in the neglect of
this duty, and so 'without God in the world'; but since,
through his forbearance and mercy, I have been in
earnest about the salvation of my own soul, and the
souls of other men, my conduct in this respect has been
very different.

'If ye, being evil, know how to give good gifts unto
your children, how much more shall your heavenly
Father give the Holy Spirit to them that ask him?' and
'If any man have not the Spirit of Christ, he is none of
his.' As he is the Spirit of truth, it is his office to lead us
into all truth, and to teach us all things; for he searches
and reveals the deep things of God. It is expressly
promised to the true church, that all her 'children shall
be taught of the Lord' (Isa. 54.13). Referring to this,
Christ has declared that none can come unto him, except
he be drawn of the Father, and taught of God (John 6.44,
45). And the apostle Paul declares, that 'the natural man
receiveth not the things of the Spirit of God; for they are
foolishness to him; neither can he know them, because
they are spiritually discerned' (1 Cor. 2.14). The natural
man [ψυχικος] is explained in Jude, by not having the
Spirit; which is evidently the apostle's meaning in this
passage; for in the preceding verse he declares that he

preached the gospel, 'not in words which man's wisdom teacheth, but which the Holy Ghost teacheth, comparing spiritual things with spiritual'. On these grounds I concluded that man's natural understanding could not, spiritually or profitably, receive the knowledge of revealed mysteries, unless it were enlightened by the Holy Spirit. I learned, also, that our eyes may be blinded by Satan, the god and prince of this world; that our understandings may be closed, and a veil be upon our hearts, when we read the Word of God; in which case the letter of the Scriptures, without the Spirit, only killeth. Hence the need of the 'understanding being opened, to understand the Scriptures'; for want of which the plainest discourses of our Lord to his disciples, concerning his sufferings, death, and resurrection, were hidden from them, and they understood them not. The veil also must be taken from the heart: for want of which the Jews, in reading the Old Testament, cannot understand the plainest declarations of Moses and the prophets, concerning their promised Saviour.

The Scriptures also everywhere declare that true wisdom is the gift of God, and must be asked of him by everyone who would be wise unto salvation; that 'the secret of the Lord is with them that fear him'; and that those who receive not the love of the truth, that they may be saved, are given over to a strong delusion, to believe a lie; that they might all be damned who believe not the truth, but have pleasure in unrighteousness (2 Thess. 2.10–12).

On these grounds, and depending upon the promises and invitations so plentifully interspersed throughout the Scriptures, when I began to inquire after the truth, I was led also in some measure to cry unto the Lord for his guidance and teaching; and as my mind grew more engaged, and my difficulties in extricating myself from the labyrinths of controversy increased, I became more and more earnest, constant, and particular, in making my requests known unto God. My constant prayer to the Lord was, to be delivered from pride and prejudice, blindness of heart, contempt of the truth, obstinacy, enthusiasm, ignorance, and error; and that the Lord would give me wisdom and knowledge, guide me to the truth as it is in Jesus, open my understanding, take away the veil from my heart, and make known unto me the way of salvation which is revealed to sinners in his Holy Word. Thus, waiting upon the Lord according to his own appointment, depending on him, and pleading his promises from day to day, I was led from one thing to another, until my view of religious truth was totally changed. This I most firmly believe to have been by the promised teaching of the Spirit of truth, powerfully enlightening my mind, opening the Scriptures, and, by dispelling the clouds of error and prejudice, enabling me to receive the truth in faith and love.

I am conscious that I have no intention, in speaking thus publicly on such a subject, but to advance the glory of God in the salvation of souls. But, as in his presence, I must declare that I have prayed over many of the most interesting passages of Scripture, chapter by chapter, and often verse by verse, with the most anxious dread of rejecting or mistaking the truth, or embracing a falsehood; and with the most earnest desire of knowing what that doctrine was which Jesus and his apostles taught. In the sight of God, I am sensible I have abundant cause to be humbled, and ashamed of my frequent remissness, and the continual defilements of my prayers; but, as surely as I believe his promises to be faithful, as surely as I believe him to be a God who hears prayer; so surely do I believe, that 'flesh and blood hath not revealed' to me the doctrines I now preach, but God himself by his Holy Spirit.

Reader, whoever thou art, if thy conscience testifies that thou hast hitherto lived in the neglect of this important duty, or the formal, lifeless, unmeaning performance of it with thy lips, while thy heart has been disengaged, and thy thoughts allowedly wandering to the ends of the earth; if thou hast not been accustomed by fervent prayer to seek wisdom from God by his teaching Spirit; if thou knowest not what it is to exercise faith upon the promises pointed out to thee, nor to plead them in prayer to a promise-keeping God; if all thy knowledge of divine things has been acquired by leaning to thy own understanding; if in reading the Scriptures thou hast looked more to learned critics, commentators, and expositors, than to the illuminating Spirit of God: then be as sure, as the Word of God is true, and as we are concerned in it, that 'the light which is in thee is darkness', and that thou 'knowest nothing yet as thou oughtest to know'. May the Lord effectually incline thine heart to take a contrary course, and to seek wisdom where alone it can be found, even from the Lord, 'the Father of lights, and the giver of every good and perfect gift', who has invited and commanded thee to ask, that it may be given thee!

6: A DISCUSSION OF ENTHUSIASM

I would observe, that there is nothing in this narrative which can reasonably be condemned as enthusiasm.

It is allowed that enthusiasm, properly so called, is a frequent attendant on religious zeal; that in some of its operations it is a grievous evil, and in all attended with many inconveniences; and that it ought very carefully to be guarded against by every religious professor and zealous preacher. It would also be in vain to pretend that the late revivals of religion, which have been indiscriminately stigmatized with the name of Methodism, have been in opinion and practice, entirely free from this enthusiasm. For what revivals of religion ever were free from scandals? Where the Lord sows his good seed, there the enemy will be sure to scatter his tares. It must be confessed, that some of the most eminent instruments in this work, whose names, when prejudice shall vanish, will be handed down with honour, as burning and shining lights, to the latest periods of the church, have, by the greatness of their zeal, through human frailty, been betrayed into sentiments, expressions, and deportment, in some instances, justly to be censured as enthusiastical; of which their enemies have not failed sufficiently to avail themselves. But whatever indiscretions and mistakes particular persons who have preached these doctrines may have fallen into, this does not, in the judgment of candid and impartial persons, in the least affect the general cause, or prove the doctrines erroneous. We would not contend for the credit of individuals, or the interests of a party, but for the doctrines of God's Word, and of the established Church of England. These will continue true and important, though many of those who have zealously and successfully preached them may have justly incurred the charge of enthusiasm: and I would confidently insist on it, that a man may be led to the belief of the doctrines, in the way of sober rational inquiry, and zealously preach them, without being an enthusiast.

It would be very well, if some of those who so readily accuse whole bodies of apparently religious persons of enthusiasm, would favour us with their determinate definition of an enthusiast. In its original meaning, the word has a very favourable sense, and implies that, by a divine influence upon the soul, a man is filled with an ardour and warmth of zeal in the cause in which he is engaged. Now 'it is good to be zealously affected always in a good thing'; and if our ardour of soul be from the Spirit of God, according to the revealed will of God, and for the glory of God, it is the noblest, most desirable, most heavenly, and most beneficial exertion of the human mind. In everything but religion, an ardour, described by the term 'enthusiasm', is allowed and commended. A poetical, a military, a patriotic enthusiasm, even when they carry men beyond the strict bounds of cold reasoning and exact prudence, fail not to meet with admirers. Our zeal may be fervent in everything without censure, unless we be zealous for the glory of God and the salvation of immortal souls. But there is an enthusiasm of this sort, which forms the highest elevation and the noblest effort of the human mind. Such an enthusiasm animated the apostle Paul in all his self-denying labours and sufferings, and filled his writings (under the guidance of the Holy Ghost) with the most ardent zeal for the honour of his dear Saviour, and affection for the souls of men. Such an enthusiasm he expresses, when he says, 'Whether we be beside ourselves, it is to God; or whether we be sober, it is for your cause: for the love of Christ constraineth us' (2 Cor. 5.13, 14). Of this enthusiasm I wish I were far more guilty.

On the other hand, there is danger of a counterfeit, pernicious enthusiasm; and about that we are at present inquiring. Now, I apprehend, that in order to constitute this culpable enthusiasm, some one or more of the following things must appear. Either, the ardour of soul excited proceeds from a heated imagination, or from a delusion of Satan, instead of being produced by a divine influence; or, the cause in which this ardour is employed is the cause of error and wickedness, instead of the cause of God and truth; or, it exerts itself in unjustifiable measures and practices. For if our ardour be warranted by the Word of God, if it do not tend to the dishonour of God, and if it be confined in its exercise to the rules and precepts of the Word of God; how intense soever it may be, I can see no cause to censure it; unless men can be too zealous for the glory of God, and the salvation of souls.

But whatever be the distinguishing criterion of enthusiasm, I suppose it will be difficult to fix a charge of it upon anything for which I plead in this narrative. I never was taught anything by impulses, impressions, visions, dreams, or revelations, except so far as the work of the Spirit in enlightening the understanding for the reception of the truths contained in the Holy Scriptures, is sometimes styled revelation. Other revelation I never expected. Not but that the Lord is sovereign, and may do what he will with his own; and, if he pleases, may, and I suppose sometimes does, go out of the ordinary course, for the conversion of a sinner, or the guidance of a perplexed, or the comfort of a distressed soul; but I never took one step in dependence on any such extra-ordinary interpositions, nor ever encouraged any person to do so. And surely it will not be called enthusiasm, by any but avowed infidels, to believe God's Word to be the standard of truth, and his promises to be faithful; and in this belief to seek for the knowledge of the doctrines of the gospel, in the manner above related. In this way I have been taught no new truths; but, as I believe, have been shown the meaning, use, tendency, consistency, harmony, wisdom, and glory of those truths which are contained in the sacred volume; but which before, through pride and ignorance, I perverted, neglected, reviled, or counted foolishness. Nor do I make any pretences to infallibility: God has not, I trust, left me so unstable, as to float about in the uncertain stream of opinion, and to be 'tossed to and fro with every wind of doctrine, by the sleight of men, and cunning craftiness, whereby they lie in wait to deceive'.

As to the grand doctrines of the gospel which I have marked out as necessary to salvation, they are neither so uncertain nor so difficult as men would persuade us. Their uncertainty and difficulty arise wholly from our pride, prejudice, love of sin, and inattentive ignorance of our own hearts. There is really much difficulty in bringing vain man to cease from leaning to his own understanding, and in prevailing with him to trust in the Lord with all his heart, and to be willing, in the humble posture of a little child, to be taught of God. Nothing but a deep conviction of guilt, a fear of wrath, and a sense of our lost condition by nature and practice, can bring our minds into this submissive frame. But, this being effected, the difficulty is over, and the way of salvation is so plain, that the 'wayfaring man, though a fool, shall not err therein'.

As to the other doctrines which I myself believe, though they seem plain enough to me, I desire not to proselyte others to them, but am willing to leave them as matters in which fallible men may differ without danger. And as to my sufficiency for the faithful dis-charge of my ministry, to God's glory and the salvation of souls, he will not, I trust, deceive my expectations, which are grounded on his promises. For the rest, I mistake daily, and find myself in continual danger of mixing my own imaginations with his divine truth, and of following my own spirit instead of his. Whatever I preach truly, or do wisely, to God be the glory; for I am not sufficient of myself to think a good thought. What-ever I speak falsely, or do foolishly, to me be the shame;

for it is the natural fruit of my own deceitful heart. If this be enthusiasm, it is an enthusiasm warranted, not only by the Word of God, as I have endeavoured to prove, but by the whole Liturgy of our Church. We all at ordination profess to be 'moved by the Holy Ghost' to take the ministerial office upon us; and assuredly we cannot be moved by the Holy Ghost, if we neither have the Holy Ghost, nor may expect his help and guidance. We agree to pray that the Lord would 'lead into the way of truth all such as have erred and are deceived'; that he would 'illuminate all bishops, priests, and deacons with true knowledge and understanding of his Holy Word'; that he would 'cleanse our hearts by the inspiration of his Holy Spirit'; that 'he would grant us true repentance and his Holy Spirit'; with much more to this effect: and I am persuaded, that such a confidence as I have expressed cannot be censured as enthusiasm, without including our Church Establishment and continual public worship in the same charge.

7: OPPONENTS SELDOM GIVE US THE HEARING

Lastly, I would observe, that our opposers and despisers will seldom give us the hearing. With all their pretensions to candour, reasoning, and free inquiry, they accuse and condemn us without so much as knowing, with any tolerable degree of accuracy, what our sentiments are, although furnished with such plentiful means of information, in those numerous publications which are now extant upon these subjects.

Having imbibed strong prejudices against us, they frame so contemptible an opinion of our understandings and writings, that they will not bestow so much pains, or afford so much regard, as to peruse our books; and to call an author a Methodist, is with many people a sufficient reason why they should not read his works. Hence it comes to pass that, for want of information, our doctrines are grievously misrepresented; and in general, the attacks made upon us, though calculated to make our persons odious and despised, do not in the least affect the argument in debate. Our adversaries in general know little of our opinions, except what they have picked up by hearsay, in which neither the connexion, consistency, tendency, nor application of those opinions is preserved; no wonder therefore that we are vilified and reproached with things to which we are utter strangers, or which we abominate and protest against every Lord's Day, and against which we neglect not to fill our writings with reasonings, warnings, and cautions.

For my own part, I freely acknowledge that my strongest objections against this scheme of doctrine arose wholly from misapprehension and mistake. Not having read their books, my notions of the doctrines of the Methodists were received from vulgar report, and from their enemies; while my creative imagination put its own construction on them, and drew terrible consequences from them: so that when I preached against them, I was as one fighting with my own shadow; and in speaking evil of those things that I knew not, I only betrayed my own ignorance and pride.

No better founded are the lamentable outcries which at this day are made against our principles, as if they tended to banish reason, argument, sober-mindedness, and morality out of the world, and in their stead to substitute a set of whimsical vagaries, which are without foundation in reason or Scripture, and have no influence, or rather a pernicious influence, in our conduct and conversation. When such a declamation is ended (for one would not interrupt it), ask the declaimer what